Catholic Ec
in the West: Roots,
Reality, and Revival

Christiaan Alting von Geusau
and Philip Booth

ACTONINSTITUTE

Christian Social Thought Series
Number 19 • Edited by Kevin Schmiesing

Christian Social Thought Series, Number 19

© 2013 by Acton Institute

All Scripture quotations are from the New American Bible, Revised Edition (NABRE).

Acton Institute
for the Study of Religion and Liberty
All rights reserved.

Cover image: Elementary students in a library classroom
© CEFutcher. Source: www.istock.com

ISBN: 978-1-938948-57-2

ACTONINSTITUTE

98 E. Fulton
Grand Rapids, Michigan 49503
Phone: 616.454.3080
Fax: 616.454.9454
www.acton.org

Printed in the United States of America

Contents

Foreword

Reform is a perennial theme in the history of Christianity. Individuals and organizations alike must constantly seek conversion—to turn away from corruption and toward Jesus Christ, the way, the truth, and the life. In the Catholic Church, monastic life, the papacy, the priesthood, and other institutions have undergone the familiar cycle: strength, followed by weakness, followed by renewal, leading again to strength.

I believe that we are in a time of renewal for an apostolate central to the preservation of the Christian faith: Catholic education. It is no secret that the period immediately following the Second Vatican Council was one of confusion in many quarters of the Church, and not least in the educational sphere. The meaning and purpose of Catholic education became muddled, even in the minds of many educators. Many times, unfortunately, teachers, professors, and administrators themselves lacked an adequate understanding of their role as evangelists charged with transmitting the faith to the next generation. Parents, who were accustomed to trusting the Church's educational institutions, too often had their trust betrayed. Parents who took seriously their primary responsibility to educate their children in the faith too often encountered opposition rather than support among Catholic schools and officials.

This occurred, ironically, in the wake of one of the finest documents ever produced on the subject, Vatican II's Declaration on Christian Education, *Gravissimum educationis*. The failure to implement fully *Gravissimum* and the consequent catechetical failures of the post-Vatican II era led, among other things, to one of the major ecclesial education projects of the twentieth century, the *Catechism of the Catholic Church*.

As this insightful work by Messrs. Alting von Geusau and Booth demonstrates, the truths embodied in *Gravissimum* and the *Catechism* are enjoying a renaissance. The authors rightly begin by stressing the indisputable focus of Catholic education: to foster the knowing and loving of Jesus Christ. To lose sight of this goal is to lose sight of the reason for Catholic schools.

The authors recognize the significant challenges that confront the renewal of Catholic education. They are well-informed concerning the political and cultural environment of the West. They are, nonetheless, hopeful that, if Catholics—parents, first and foremost—reassert their role as guardians of the faith of their children, then Catholic education will once again become a beacon of excellence and a source of sanctity for the Church and the world. Catholics and other Christians, laypeople and clergy alike, would do well to take to heart the guidance contained in this wise volume.

+Christoph Cardinal Schönborn
Archbishop of Vienna, Austria

1   Introduction

Catholic education is a vast topic vastly misunderstood. Were one to ask a parent or teacher from any Western country what they consider to be the most important hallmark of the Catholic schools and universities that they know, likely answers would be "academic quality," "inclusiveness" or the school being "value-oriented." These aspects are, indeed, all very important, but they are not what a Catholic educational institution is primarily about. If it were, then little would distinguish a Catholic institution from many of its secular counterparts. There is, or should be, much more about Catholic education than meets the modern eye.

This monograph seeks to contribute to a deeper understanding of the nature of Catholic education, to analyse the current unsatisfying state of affairs in Catholic education in the West as a whole, and to propose possible solutions as we move forward. Discussions about education policy at government level are informed by the foundational principles of Catholic social teaching and the particular way in which these foundational principles have been applied in documents published by the Church on the subject of education. This discussion is related to practice in a number of Western countries and policy conclusions are suggested.

However, though the public policy environment is important, simply ensuring that we have the right government policies in place is no guarantee of an education system fit for the purpose of educating and forming today's young Catholics. Catholics themselves must take responsibility. As Catholics, we should already know what we are looking for: "The kind of education we want is one that fits us to know the truth that will set us free."[1] It is Christ, who is the way, the truth and the life, who will set us free. Christ should thus be the centre of any Catholic educational initiative. Indeed, during one of his first public appearances after being elected pope in 2005, Benedict XVI, commenting on the outpouring of love for the deceased Blessed John Paul II by youth around the world, dispelled the notion that the young are only superficial and materialistic. To the contrary, he said, "They want great things, good things. This is why young people are—you are—once again fully open to Christ."[2]

---

[1] Stratford Caldecott, *Beauty in the Word: Rethinking the Foundations of Education* (Tacoma, WA: Angelico Press, 2012), 8.

[2] Address of Pope Benedict XVI to German pilgrims (25 April 2005).

II   What Is Catholic Education?

A regeneration of Christian culture is not only possible, says
Catholic author and artist Michael O'Brien, it is our responsibility. This is so, he says, because "we bear witness to the
greatest story of all" that in the words of Chesterton "fulfils
man's greatest needs."[1] Catholic education, then, supporting
parents in their role as the primary educators of their children,
should aim to fulfil these needs; it can only do so when the
story is told in the right way. Catholic education, in the words
of Benedict XVI to educators in Washington, DC, in 2008,
should first and foremost be a place where "we encounter the
living God who in Jesus Christ reveals his transforming love and
truth."[2] Here we have a very clear definition that leaves little
doubt as to what the core message of every Catholic school
and university should be. Curtis Hancock says the same in a
different way: "For the Christian, then, God is the Alpha and
Omega of education, a fact that gives the Christian knowledge
and *wisdom*."[3]

---

[1]   Michael D. O'Brien, *A Landscape with Dragons: The Battle for Your
Child's Mind* (San Francisco, CA: Ignatius Press 1998), 117.

[2]   Pope Benedict XVI, Address during meeting with Catholic educators,
Washington, DC (17 April 2008).

[3]   Curtis L. Hancock, *Recovering a Catholic Philosophy of Elementary
Education* (Pine Beach, NJ: Newman House Press, 2005), 43.

How seriously do we take this profound understanding of Catholic education in the West today? Do students really encounter the living God in our Catholic schools and universities and are Christ's love and truth indeed revealed to them in the classroom, the hallway and the library, let alone the chapel if it has not been turned into a "meditation room" or "multi-faith centre"? Are students introduced to the Word of God or to the word of secularism? Do they even know the difference? Are they fitted to deal with secularism, both in discourse with their neighbour and in its more aggressive form in the political sphere? Is God indeed the Alpha and Omega of our Catholic institutions of education? Do we take the words of Pope Benedict as literally as they are meant to be, or do we—publicly or privately—say that this is indeed a worthy ideal but hardly attainable in our secular and pluralistic society? After all, "we can't impose our views" and the state—which is often funding Catholic schools and universities—demands what it describes as a "neutral" worldview.

During the past decades many—perhaps the majority—of those involved in Catholic education have compromised heavily the Christian identity and principles of their schools and universities because adhering to the rules for state funding have forced them to do so. They may have done so willingly or reluctantly, implicitly or explicitly, but the effect is the same. It is vital for the Catholic school to have a great deal of independence from the state to pursue a mission that is truly Catholic in all aspects and that treats the person as a whole and not as separate compartments each of which is educated according to different philosophies.

A more prevalent reason for the dramatic decline in Catholic identity is, however, the lack of faith formation and personal conviction of the faculty and leadership of many Catholic educational institutions. This decline has led to a Catholic population in the West today that, for the most part, is well-meaning but little (in)formed about the faith and its eternal wisdom. We see this development in spite of the fact that the Catholic Church and Catholics as such possess all the content, tools, and experience to offer the best possible education and human formation. The success of those educational institutions that have retained an uncompromised Catholic identity and mission are proof of the validity of Pope Benedict's exhortation and the Church's unrelenting teaching on this subject. Wherever it is applied consistently, the Catholic model of education throughout its long history has proven to be very successful.

Whilst the parent is the prime educator of children, the Catholic nature of a school does not depend on the number of children who are Catholic. The Catholic school and university can be a place of mission and must be a place of evangelisation of both Catholic and non-Catholic students. Of course, the student body—and parents where relevant—must be open to places of education that pursue this role, but the key issue is the leadership, faculty, and teachers of the school or college.

In order to allow the encounter of God and Man to take place in education as Pope Benedict suggests, we may distinguish three pillars on which institutions for Catholic education should rest, and three objectives that should be pursued by those developing the pillars.

The Three Pillars

For education to be truly Catholic and whole, schools and universities identifying themselves as such should be solidly founded on three pillars: the Word of God, the Magisterium of the Church, and the sacramental life of the Church. The unity of these three in education, guided by a life of prayer in and around the school, is essential to the viability of the school's Catholic identity and formative role. This unity will ensure that education leads to the beauty of wisdom by accepting and feeding our desire to know truth and to see reality for what it is. Through such education, we allow Christ to be placed at the centre of life and to be the light that shines on all we need to know in order to understand the nature and purpose of human life.

Scripture is the best possible handbook for Catholic education because it tells us in detail why and where we are called to educate and how it should be done. Christ himself calls directly upon his followers to educate the world. We read in Mark 16:15: "Go into the whole world and proclaim the gospel to every creature." In Matthew 28:19–20 we are told: "Go, therefore, and make disciples of all nations, baptising them in the name of the Father, and of the Son, and of the Holy Spirit, teaching them to observe all that I have commanded you."

These passages are not, as is often misunderstood, limited to the call to dispatch brave missionaries to preach the Gospel in far-flung countries amongst heathen tribes. They are demanding more than that: They comprise an assignment to teach the *whole* of humanity the Gospel in full, to educate *all* peoples. Pope Francis underlined this in his homily to over three million people gathered in Rio de Janeiro during the closing Mass of World Youth Day 2013:

> Where does Jesus send us? There are no borders, no limits: he sends us to everyone. The Gospel is for everyone, not just for some. It is not only for those who seem closer to us, more receptive, more welcoming. It is for everyone. Do not be afraid to go and to bring Christ into every area of life, to the fringes of society, even to those who seem farthest away, most indifferent. The Lord seeks all, he wants everyone to feel the warmth of his mercy and his love.[4]

---

[4] Holy Mass for the 28th World Youth Day (Rio de Janeiro, 28 July 2013), available at http://www.vatican.va.

We need to be reminded at this point that Scripture is not just a lofty code of conduct that applies to certain people and certain situations only: It is concerned with all human persons and all aspects of human existence. The core of the Church's primary mission to evangelise is therefore to educate. Education is fundamental to evangelisation. It is for good reason that, throughout history, missionaries, monasteries and dioceses have founded churches with schools directly attached to them, because, as Christians, we believe that the Word of God and the life of the Church inform all we are and all we do.

Pope Benedict stresses to Catholic educators that "*each and every aspect* of your learning communities reverberates within the ecclesial life of faith."[5] This is not therefore a matter of selection, of choosing those elements of Catholicity that happen to fit with personal preferences or with current trends in education and in society. It is a far more radical demand because it requires from teachers and administrators that: "public witness to the way of Christ, as found in the Gospel and upheld by the Church's Magisterium, shapes all aspects of an institution's life, both inside and outside the classroom." Benedict goes on to say that "divergence from this vision weakens Catholic identity and, far from advancing freedom, inevitably leads to confusion, whether moral, intellectual or spiritual."[6] The practical and daily consequences of such an approach are well described in Patrick O'Donoghue's much commented and highly praised manual *Fit for Mission? Schools* in which the former Bishop of Lancaster describes step-by-step how this public witness to Christ in Catholic schools should be

---

[5] Pope Benedict XVI, Address during meeting with Catholic educators, Washington, DC (17 April 2008) (emphasis added).

[6] Pope Benedict XVI, Address during meeting with Catholic educators.

implemented as it seeks to "renew the gospel fire dampened by the secular agenda."[7]

Leaving no aspect unattended, therefore, education should be comprehensively grounded in the unity of the Word of God, the Church's teaching, and the sacraments. We can already read this requirement in the Old Testament in Deuteronomy 6:5, and it is repeated as the first commandment by Jesus in the gospel of Mark 12:30: "You shall love the Lord your God with all your heart, with all your soul, with all your mind, and with all your strength" (see also, Matt. 22:37 and Luke 10:27). Jesus refers here to all our human faculties and characteristics—not just to our heart and soul but also to our minds that should love and follow him in all we do.

Paul says in 2 Corinthians 10:4–5 that our every thought should be taken captive in obedience to Christ and because education is about thinking, it should also take place in obedience to Christ. Douglas Wilson, in his brilliant book on Christian education, further expands Paul's exhortation where he says that the Word of God "is the light in which we see and understand everything else." Without God, Wilson goes on to say, the universe is a fragmented pile of incomprehensible particulars.[8] Stratford Caldecott rightly notes how without this light "[O]ur curricula have become fragmented and incoherent because we have lost any sense of how all knowledge fits together."[9] Wilson uses a powerful image, in which the sun represents God, to highlight this point: "The Christian educa-

---

[7] Patrick O'Donoghue, *Fit for Mission? Schools: See with His Eyes, Love with His heart, Share in His Virtues*, expanded ed. (London, UK: Catholic Truth Society, 2008), 7.

[8] Douglas Wilson, *Recovering the Lost Tools of Learning: An Approach to Distinctively Christian Education* (Wheaton, IL: Crossway Books 1991), 59.

[9] Caldecott, *Beauty in the Word*, 8.

tor's job is not to require the students to spend all their time gazing at the sun. Rather, we want them to examine everything else in the light the sun provides."[10] In Catholic education, the understanding of man and the universe is therefore made visible through this light of the Word of God, aided by the Magisterium and nourished by the sacraments. This light permeates the whole of the curriculum and all the school undertakes. The Eucharist should have a prominent place in the life of the school as it is here that the student's and the teacher's heart is prepared for a real encounter with Christ himself. This encounter offers the possibility of seeing the world through the eyes of a loving God, allowing for the truth to be seen in creation itself.

In Catholic education, everything is thus considered through Christ as Master of the universe and all that is within it. In the Old Testament, we are already being told that God's Word and his commandments should be the light that shines on all that we do and wherever we go. Returning to Deuteronomy 6 again, we read in verses 6–9:

> Take to heart these words which I command you today. Keep repeating them to your children. Recite them when you are at home and when you are away, when you lie down and when you get up. Bind them on your arm as a sign and let them be as a pendant on your forehead. Write them on the doorposts of your houses and on your gates.

The point being made here is this: Catholic education cannot be seen in any other way than as the faith itself, namely that Christ is the beginning, the way, and the end of everything in life. Without this central premise—and recognition of the teaching authority of the Church Christ established and its sacramental mission—education cannot be Catholic. It is the

[10] Wilson, *Recovering the Lost Tools of Learning*, 63.

totality of the faith integrated with the educational project that counts. What distinguishes a Catholic school from a secular school is the guiding light chosen to lead the educational endeavour. In the former, it is God the creator of heaven and earth himself; in the latter it is all too likely to be the god of secularism, thinly disguised as a so-called "neutral worldview."

Because education is all about teaching the young mind how to think about the world and how to understand and deal with it, neutrality of worldview is not possible. When children are formed to take their places in the world, they need to learn to make choices based on an inner conviction. This is hardly a neutral affair. Rather, when the neutrality mantra is brought forward, it is in truth something very different that is being proposed by stealth. Far from what is claimed, secularism is not neutral when it rejects the light of Christ or any other religious inspiration. It is merely offering a rival faith that we all too often ignore for what it is. The very rejection of the concept of "absolute truth" itself assumes an absolute truth. Unfortunately, this rival faith of secularism has increasingly taken over Catholic schools dependent on government funding or led by lukewarm Catholics and therefore no longer willing or able to keep out the non-Christian worldview. In John 14:6, Jesus makes it clear that for his followers, in whatever they do, there is no room for neutrality: "I am the way and the truth and the life. No one comes to the Father except through me." We have to choose and there is no middle road available. The mission of Catholic education is defined and illuminated by this key gospel verse.

The Three Objectives

Catholic educational institutions should have three goals in order to be able to fulfil their primary missions to allow students to "encounter the living God who in Jesus Christ reveals his transforming love and truth." These objectives are (1) to provide an environment in which students are enabled to build and deepen their relationship with God, (2) to foster an academic culture aimed at the pursuit of truth, and (3) to actively promote growth in virtue.

In his latest book *Jesus of Nazareth: The Infancy Narratives*, Benedict XVI provides the ideal background for the first two of these objectives where he makes two crucial observations.[11] The first point is that man is a relational being.[12] When the most fundamental of these relationships—man's relation to God—is disturbed then nothing else in life can be truly in order, even when the illusion persists that all is well and good. The second relevant observation is that being a Christian means deliberately moving away from that which everyone thinks or wants, in order to separate oneself from the prevailing standards. We need to be willing to focus on what lies outside the realm "of what is important and powerful in worldly terms." This attitude is needed in order to enter into the light of the truth of our being so that we may steer onto the right path of a life in Christ.[13] Our educational endeavours, therefore, should not be guided by public opinion but by the (at times inconvenient) truth of God's created order. Ratzinger's thoughts lead us to understand that fostering a personal relationship with God and allowing for the truth to shine its light on every aspect of human life are essential to Catholic education. Catholic education is meant to allow the student to come to know Christ and through this relationship be able to better understand and deal with the reality of the natural created order.

---

[11] Josef Ratzinger [Pope Benedict XVI], *Jesus of Nazareth: The Infancy Narratives* (New York: Image, 2012).

[12] Ratzinger, *Jesus of Nazareth*, 44.

[13] Ratzinger, *Jesus of Nazareth*, 66–67.

When Christ is the centre of all we do, then we are enabled to redirect our focus of life towards an understanding of the world in which we live that is geared towards the promotion of human dignity and the common good. Young men and women graduating from Catholic schools and universities should have the keen understanding of being called as Christians to work for the common good and to do so through a life that is deeply rooted in Christ, combined with a vigorous desire to pursue the truth of things, to live through and with reality rather than merely being guided by constantly changing feelings and preferences.

It is at this point that the primary importance of what we would call "virtue-oriented" formation becomes visible. Virtues are so much more important than values because virtues are part of the law written into the human heart: the natural law. Values, on the other hand, tend to be human-made and change-able and therefore, although still important, stand on less solid ground. An exception should be made here for what Marcus Stock refers to as the "Gospel values" in education. These are the Beatitudes summarised in values that Catholic schools should teach.[14] The Beatitudes, being proclaimed by Christ himself, are, in fact, a more detailed expression of how the virtues should be lived in practice. Catholic schools should let the educational endeavour be guided by a constant promotion of the virtues, especially the cardinal virtues of prudence, justice, fortitude, and temperance.

Prudence, the philosopher Josef Pieper says, is the "mother" of all virtues because it precedes and measures them: all virtue is necessarily prudent.[15] Prudence is the virtue that applies

---

[14] Marcus Stock, *Christ at the Centre: Why the Church Provides Catholic Schools*, 2nd ed. (London, UK: Catholic Truth Society, 2012), 16.

[15] Josef Pieper, *The Four Cardinal Virtues* (Notre Dame, IN: University of Notre Dame Press, 1966), 3, 5.

the knowledge of reality to do what is good. Its aim is truth in all. Justice is the virtue that leads us to what is right so that "man give[s] man what is his due."[16] Fortitude is more than just bravery: It is the willingness to suffer injuries or even death in the pursuit or defence of the good. It is the willingness to expose oneself for the sake of truth. Temperance is the virtue that recognises the inner order of man and leads to the willingness to shape one's life according to it, requiring selflessness and sacrifice. Humility, gentleness, and chastity are but some of the realisations of temperance.[17]

No matter how strong the faith of a person might be, without a certain degree of practice in the virtues, it will be hard not to be led exclusively by the emotions and impressions that constantly enter our minds. A necessary part of an education that leads students to live by truth and love rather than by feeling or opinion is to help them attain and strengthen the exercise of these virtues so that their learning process is not hampered by a self-created haze. Catholic education should be such that it "leads us to truth and wisdom, to right order and virtue."[18]

Pope Emeritus Benedict fittingly calls it the duty of the educator to be led by "intellectual charity" that is inspired by the recognition that leading the young to truth is an act of love.[19] Thus, in Catholic education, to paraphrase James Schall, there should be an intimate and dynamic connection between the moral life and the intellectual life.[20] It is so that this connection exists and persists that the training in the

---

[16] Pieper, *Four Cardinal Virtues*, 44.

[17] See Pieper, *Four Cardinal Virtues*, 150, 151

[18] James V. Schall, *Liberal Learning* (Wilmington, DE: ISI Books, 2000), 47.

[19] Benedict XVI, Address during his meeting with Catholic educators, Washington, DC (17 April 2008).

[20] Schall, *Liberal Learning*, 30.

virtues is so important. What has gone so sadly wrong in Catholic education in the post-War Western world is that this connection has been mostly lost whilst the virtues needed to establish and uphold it have been largely ignored (see chapter 3). A majority of Catholic schools and universities has over the past decades moved ever closer to the mainstream relativistic and secular standards of education, and in the process they have lost their distinctive character of integrally forming human beings through the light of Christ. Most schools and universities calling themselves "Catholic" nowadays have more in common with secular skills-oriented and neutral-worldview education than with the Catholic tradition of the formation of the whole human being in the light of Christ: an education that is focused on *the meaning of life* and driven by the attainment of virtues. The prevalent secular form of education is described well by R. J. Rushdoony as "the enthronement of anti-meaning."[21] Catholic education is meant to be the exact opposite of that. True Catholic formation is all about meaning and prepares a person to be a Christian in the world.

Rushdoony goes even further and observes that education is in fact religion—whether a civic state-sponsored religion such as the secularism described above or a church-inspired religion:

> If education is in any sense a preparation for life, then its concern is religious. If education is at all concerned with truth, it is again religious. If education is vocational, then it deals with calling, a basically religious concept. It would be absurd to reduce preparation for life, truth and calling to an exclusively religious meaning in any parochial sense, but it is obvious that these and

---

[21] R. J. Rushdoony, *The Messianic Character of American Education* (Portland, OR: Ross House Books, 1995), 312.

other aspects of education are inescapably religious. As Whitehead observed, "The essence of education is that it be religious."[22]

Here we touch again on the fallacy discussed above, namely the modern conviction that education should be neutral and devoid of any moral framework, let alone religion. The relativistic mindset that reigns at most schools and universities, including many of those calling themselves Catholic, proclaiming that all truths are equal and the secular truth "more equal" than others, tells us that religion and education need to be separated because they have nothing to do with each other. Religion is relegated to the exclusivity of the private and entirely autonomous sphere of mere opinion. Nonsecular religion is simply seen as the free exercise of such a private opinion and the freedom to worship that happens to come with it. As Rushdoony convincingly points out, there is in fact no major aspect of education that does not have a religious connotation. What is really being proposed by secularist movements is that the pupil should replace whatever god he believes in with the secular god. Catholic educators however should be able to identify this ruse and know that the only proper way to educate is by providing a formation that centres on Christ alone. It is the only way to enable the student to beat out a coherent path of life by being guided by the one and only God who created heaven and earth.

The call to the New Evangelisation as initiated by Blessed John Paul II and continued under Pope Benedict XVI and Pope Francis has everything to do with Catholic education and its fundamental religious orientation. The "List of Propositions" published by the Synod of Bishops in October 2012 summarises

---

[22] Rushdoony, *Messianic Character*, 315.

well this intricate connection between educating, faith and evangelising:

> Education is a constitutive dimension of evangelization. To proclaim the Risen Jesus Christ is to accompany all human beings in their personal story, in their development and in their spiritual vocation. Education needs, at the same time, to promote everything that is true, good and beautiful that is a part of the human person, that is to say, to educate the mind and the emotions to appreciate reality. Children, teenagers and young people have a right to be evangelized and educated. The schools and Catholic universities respond in this way to this need.[23]

In order for Christians to be able to promote effectively the true, the good, and the beautiful, both where it concerns the faith in general as well as with regard to Catholic education specifically, there is the vital need for coherence in word and deed. Pope Paul VI brought this strikingly to the point when he observed that "(M)odern man listens more willingly to witnesses than to teachers, and if he does listen to teachers, it is because they are witnesses."[24] Modern man, being increasingly nonreligious, is especially intolerant of hypocrisy where it comes to faith and morals, and the failure of many Catholic educators to live the gospel and the sacramental life of the Church whilst teaching and leading schools and universities has done great harm to the cause of Catholic education. This means that the Catholic educator has to visibly strive for perfection in Christ as he exhorts us to do: "So be perfect, just as your heavenly Father is perfect" (Matt. 5:48). The Catholic

---

[23] Proposition 27, XIII Ordinary General Assembly of the Synod of Bishops (7–28 October 2012): The New Evangelization for the Transmission of the Christian Faith.

[24] Pope Paul VI, Apostolic Exhortation *Evangelii Nuntiandi* (8 December 1975), no. 41.

novelist Michael D. O'Brien powerfully expresses how words can never be separated from the life of the person speaking them: "[...] a messenger is in his words, if the messenger is truly himself. His life is his primary word, and his spoken words bear his life. He learns to be this when he has discovered that a man can give to others only what he truly is."[25]

Young people are especially sensitive to this for they are shaped more by the concrete experiences in their lives, and thus the lived example of their teachers, than by the best of pedagogical techniques.[26] Charles Chaput in this context says about Catholic education: "God renews the world with our actions, not our intentions. What separates real discipleship from surface piety is whether we actually do what we say we believe."[27] Any form of Catholic education will ultimately fail when the student is confronted with the word being spoken not conforming to the life being lived.

Summary

From the above, three things are clear. The Catholic school and university must be integrally Catholic. It must involve the Christian formation of the whole person: physical, intellectual, spiritual and social. It can only do so when its teachers and leadership themselves have lives deeply rooted in Christ. This applies in general to Christian life and to the effectiveness of the New Evangelisation: only when the Word is visibly lived

---

[25] Michael D. O'Brien, *Island of the World* (San Francisco: Ignatius Press 2007), 796.

[26] See J. Michael Miller, *The Holy See's Teaching on Catholic Schools* (Atlanta: Solidarity Association, 2006), 56–59, for a more detailed discussion on this point.

[27] Charles J. Chaput, Catholic Schools and the Christian Mission (January 30, 2013), 1, available at http://www.zenit.org/en.

by the one who speaks it can it have any effect at all. As Saint Francis put it so well: "Preach the Gospel but only use words when strictly necessary."

The context within which education is provided will, of course, determine what is taught and how it is taught. One should not think of Catholic education as something that is only available to the academically gifted. In general, a distinction is often made between education and professional training or vocational studies. The former involves, it is thought, the training of the mind and the latter often involves the more direct development of what is often called "human capital" for some practical purpose.

It is generally thought that an academic education requires immersion in Christian principles and Catholic life but, for example, training to be a plumber or a car mechanic does not. However, this distinction ignores the primary call of Christian life, which is, as Pope Benedict fittingly says, to "immerse one's life in Christ." This means that every aspect of life—as has already been discussed in detail above—should be guided by a Christian ethos, whether one is receiving a general education or preparing for a specific professional career or trade.

Although this monograph focuses on general education, it should be underlined that its principles are equally applicable to professional and vocational training, be it within a different context. The call to holiness is not limited to the priest or the theology professor; it is equally relevant for the pilot or the bus driver. As we have seen, it is not the teaching of skills that should take precedent, but rather the person's ability to make reasoned decisions within the framework of the natural and moral order that is illuminated by a life in Christ and his Church. Somebody who wishes to follow a specific professional or vocational course will, as they get older, be exposed to more practical skills in their chosen field. That person must also be able to make right judgements both in the context of work and in life more generally. His earlier formative education will be important in helping him make those judgements, but a training of Christian character might also be as important as the practical skills that are taught more directly. This is obvious in vocations such as nursing or teaching, in which skills there have always been Catholic places of training. Recent events in the world economy and financial markets demonstrate that there is also a great need for this way of thinking in the teaching of finance and business studies. There are many other areas of training for which this could be said, for example, medicine and law. The fact is that, for Christians, nothing that they do or learn should remain unaffected by their faith in Christ.

III   The Rise and Decline of Catholic Education

As we discussed in detail in chapter 2, education has been part of the Church's mission ever since Christ called on his followers to fulfil this specific task. Jesus himself was an educator *par excellence*, spending most of his time during his public ministry teaching his disciples and the massive crowds he attracted on a wide array of topics. Jesus taught the gospel not merely as a lofty code of conduct, but as a way of life, as a light meant to shine on all we think and do. Of course, education as such is as old as humanity itself. Parents have always educated their children, albeit in very different ways. Such parental education ranged from the passing on of oral traditions from generation to generation to the father of Wolfgang Amadeus Mozart teaching his children reading, writing, mathematics, and literature during the many months the family spent travelling in a carriage through Europe. In spite of the strong opposition to the idea of homeschooling one encounters in many Western (especially European) countries today, it was the choice form of education throughout human history both before and after the Church and the state became involved. The ruling classes, to whom education was mostly limited until the Middle Ages, almost exclusively homeschooled with parents, family members, and tutors teaching all subjects. The idea of it being expected of good citizens to send their children out of the family house to be educated by complete strangers is relatively new in human history.[1] This should not be forgotten and might help us understand that, when it comes to the concept of universal education through organised schools, we are, historically speaking, still in an early phase of its development—or perhaps, indeed, the trend towards education through schooling will reverse.

Some Historical Considerations

Organised Catholic education by way of the founding and leading of schools is a development that is closely linked to the rise of monasticism from the third century onwards. Anthony of Egypt (251–356), one of the fathers of early Christian monasticism, did not found the first Catholic school in the Egyptian desert, but through the tradition he started monasteries throughout Europe rapidly developed into important centres of research and learning and in times of upheaval served as the depositories of Western culture and tradition. Soon, monks throughout Europe would be sharing the results of their arduous study with students who were not part of the monastic community. This would lead in the later Middle Ages to monasteries becoming, with the exception of the bishops and their cathedral schools, the primary providers of education through extended libraries, schools, and universities. Until the early Middle Ages, formal education had been mostly limited to the ruling classes and clergy, and it was only through the educational revival of the twelfth century that education became more widely available. Later, religious orders were founded and continue to exist today with the specific mission to provide

---

[1] Most Western countries have laws that are frequently described as requiring "compulsory education." In fact, it is "schooling" that is generally compulsory. It is possible to attend school without becoming educated or to be educated without attending school.

education. Such orders include the Salesians and the Piarists as well as the Jesuits and the Dominicans. The great mediaeval universities of Paris, Bologna, Oxford, and Cambridge were all founded through the active involvement of the Catholic Church, its clergy and religious orders. Even the colonists on the American continent started founding Catholic schools and universities as early as the beginning of the sixteenth century. Until the end of the eighteenth century, education on any level in Europe—at least outside Russia, Scandinavia, England, and Scotland—was for the most part run by the Catholic Church and its congregations.

As Christopher Dawson points out in his monumental work on the crisis of Western education, there was a remarkable unity in the educational development of the West from the fourth century until the seventeenth, during which the prevalence of the two great traditions of Christianity and classical culture remained constant, despite many different approaches being applied throughout this long period.[2] This started changing gradually with the onset of the Reformation and the division it caused within Christianity.

The unity of Christianity and classical culture in education broke down further with the vast new horizons that opened up for humanity as the age of discoveries came to new heights in the seventeenth and eighteenth centuries. The Renaissance and the increasing importance of mechanical and purely scientific knowledge rather than scholarly study led to a radically different orientation in education throughout Europe. The Church increasingly lost influence in the great educational institutions it had created, partly because it was often unable to articulate effectively its answers to the rapidly changing realities and the onset of secularisation. By the time the French

---

[2] See Christopher Dawson, *The Crisis of Western Education* (Washington, DC: The Catholic University of America Press 2010 [1961]), 33.

Revolution overtook France in 1789, the established Catholic schools and universities there had little strength and support left to defend their educational model and unique position in society. They lost all their privileges and financial support structures overnight and were closed down en masse by the new revolutionary regime. It is often conveniently forgotten that, as Dawson describes it: "[N]ever, not even at the Reformation or the Russian Revolution, was there such a wholesale slaughter of educational institutions."[3] After the revolution there would be no functioning educational system in France until Napoleon came to power and introduced a strongly state-controlled school and university system. It would be the beginning of the emergence of centralised government systems of education as we know them today in the West, inspired by a drive for nationalisation and secularisation that has sometimes decelerated—at least in some countries—but has generally been unrelenting.

Although the history of Catholic education in the Anglo-American world did not see this drive for state centralisation start as early as the eighteenth century, the twentieth century did bring on this development as well, be it in different forms and not always intentionally. Still, thanks to the more deeply rooted tradition of private educational initiative in English-speaking countries, the United States has a much broader field of independent Catholic schools and universities than many countries in continental Europe. Both systems however suffered equally from this decline in Catholic education, which intensified after the Second World War.

It is worth stressing again that this decline in Catholic education and rise of the state's role was not even across time and across all countries. In the United Kingdom, for example, the vast majority of Catholic children can attend Catholic schools without any significant discrimination in the way in which they

---

[3] Dawson, *Crisis of Western Education*, 43.

are funded compared with secular schools, but those schools are heavily controlled by the government and parental autonomy is limited. In the United States, private schools are numerous and relatively free of state control, but Catholic parents are taxed without receiving state support to send their children to Catholic schools on the same basis as secular schools are funded. In some countries, the curriculum and admissions policies are controlled and, in others, homeschooling prohibited. These differences are discussed in greater detail in chapter 5.

Root Causes of the Decline

The underlying cause of the decline is clearly rooted in the process of secularisation that started in earnest during the second half of the eighteenth century in Europe. As the religious traditions on which Western civilization was founded continue to be shed on all levels of society, the West has become almost exclusively focused on organising the world according to its democratic, scientific, and economic models. Descartes in the seventeenth century already strived for the utilitarian ideal (also to be firmly instilled in education) that human progress, especially through the development of science, should lead to the human race's becoming "the masters and possessors of nature,"[4] thus leaving out the Creator. The eighteenth-century enlightenment rationalism of Kant and his followers was instrumental in basically replacing God as the ultimate end with the absolute individual autonomy of practical reason. These developments have led to a modern culture devoid of any religious principles and as a result increasingly at odds with or even hostile towards the rest of the world, in particular the Catholic Church. Modern culture is not pluralistic and tolerant as it claims to be. It is the opposite, as Dawson summarises

---

[4] See also Dawson, *Crisis of Western Education*, 40.

pointedly: "it is more unitary, more uniform and more highly centralized and organized than any culture that the world has known hitherto."[5]

The combination of modern universal education with the rapid developments in global mass communication, have moved young and old alike into the orbit of the unitary secular culture. Opposing or even questioning this culture in any way is regarded as a rejection of universal human progress and therefore considered unacceptable. Few are able to see through the thin screen of false peace created by this highly centralised society where individual initiative and personal responsibility are little stimulated lest they become a threat to the uniform civil order imposed from above, especially where it concerns education. Once again Pope Benedict points us to the core of the problem, which constitutes a flight from responsibility due to the lack of a coherent moral order for Western society to live by: "There is a need to renounce that false peace promised by the idols of this world along with the dangers which accompany it, that false peace which dulls consciences, which leads to self-absorption, to a withered existence lived in indifference."[6] There are various ways in which, as a result of the developments described here, Catholic education has steadily declined in Western societies as well. We can think of four distinct (though certainly related) aspects of the decline.

First, and most importantly, there is the decline in interest in and support for properly-Catholic education amongst Catholic families themselves. The decline is mostly due to the general de-Christianisation of Western society as described above, whereby in most cases the Catholic faith is no longer actively transmitted by parents to their children. Church at-

---

[5] Dawson, *Crisis of Western Education*, 111–12.

[6] Pope Benedict XVI, Message for the celebration of the World Day of Peace (1 January 2013).

tendance has been dwindling since the end of World War II, and families are breaking apart in ever-larger numbers.[7] This has led to vocations into the priesthood and the religious life decreasing dramatically too. The long chain of passing on the faith and its wisdom from generation to generation has finally been broken and only minorities of practising Catholics remain. Where there is no living faith in Catholic families, first the parishes dwindle, then the local Catholic schools decline, followed by the collapse of traditional marriage and vocations to religious life. This has, in turn, led to religious orders and dioceses no longer being able to provide sufficient well-trained Catholic personnel and the financial means for the schools they have run for centuries. Without a substantial number of intact Catholic families, no Church structure can survive, especially in education, as they are run by and financed through those individuals who have grown up in such families.

Second, and this is closely related to the first point, there is a serious lack of certified teachers with a Catholic formation and equipped with the personal conviction and example of a Christian life necessary for the school to uphold a Catholic identity and tradition and transmit this effectively to its students. Throughout the Western world, we see many schools and universities that are still Catholic in name and image but lack the appropriate identity and mission. Due to the situation described above, finding teachers who live the faith and have the desire to pass it on to their pupils is increasingly difficult. Additionally, many of these teachers themselves received their professional formation at state-run secular schools and universities and therefore do not know what Catholic education

---

[7] This statement is true as a generalization across Western nations, even if it does not account for relatively minor differences and variations among countries, such as the increase in church attendance in the United States during the 1950s.

entails in its entirety. Without receiving a thorough Catholic formation in the family, it is difficult—though not, of course, impossible—to have at least received a general sense of what is required of them. Even here only very few would be sufficiently aware of the full meaning and implications of a Catholic education where "we encounter the living God who in Jesus Christ reveals his transforming love and truth." Related to this is the tendency to see Catholic education as desirable for its (often) superior academic quality rather than because of the quality of the human and religious formation young people receive through such education and the unique sort of Catholic teachers this requires (though this is probably more the case in Europe and the United Kingdom than in the United States).

Third, the decline in support for Catholic schools and universities has also involved a decline in their financial viability. Support from religious orders and parishes for Catholic education has often dwindled, not least because of the decrease in vocations to consecrated religious life, which previously had been the primary source of personnel for staffing Catholic schools. Therefore, where the state has stepped in with financial support, the quid pro quo has been a high level of state control. If the state provides no support for Catholic parents to send children to the school of their choice, but continues to tax the population to finance education (and other aspects of the welfare state), a particularly large financial commitment is needed for parents to send their children to fully independent private Catholic schools out of smaller net incomes. In other countries, effective control of Catholic (private) schools is exercised by the state (often with the willing cooperation of the ecclesial authorities).[8] This development has led in

---

8 Both the point about the emphasis on academic quality made earlier and that of the Church's being happy—indeed enthusiastic—to cede control to the state is illustrated in the joint Bishops' Pastoral letter on

many countries to a system of Catholic education that owes its existence to the state entirely and therefore cannot veer off from the centralised educational structure and strictly secular curriculum in which there is little room, if any, for a strong Catholic identity and therefore a Christ-centred education (see chapter 5). State money—especially where it is directed through institutions and not through parents—can, in fact, largely take away the independence and uniquely Christian character from Catholic schools and universities.

This leads to the fourth problem. Governments have exercised increasing control of curricula and teaching personnel and there is increasing pressure on governments to remove the independence of Catholic schools. Sometimes this comes under the guise of pressure to remove any state funding for religious schools on the ground that religion should be a private matter and have no connection with state funding. More directly, it can be an attack on school and family autonomy arising from the erroneous belief that all children in a society should be given the same state-designed curriculum that has no religious grounding and is misleadingly presented as "morally neutral."

---

education in England and Wales in which it is stated (2 September 2007):

> Recent and current calls from some for the abolition of faith schools, or their curtailment, fail to take account of this rich history of co-operation between Church and State which has been to the mutual benefit of both. They also fail to take account of the current achievements of our schools. Independent research and inspection conducted by the Government's own offices demonstrate how well our schools perform, academically and in moral and social education.

The ordering of words may or may not be significant here but one also has to question whether the "Government's own offices" are well equipped to make a judgement on moral education except where this involves the most generalised moral norms.

As we discussed above, this is of course merely the imposition of another religion: that of secularism.

This perspective reaches its zenith in totalitarian states, but it is worth noting that, even in modern-day Germany, the ban on homeschooling that was implemented in 1938 still exists, with more or less the same justification, namely that the state should have the final say in all matters pertaining to the education of children. The same limitations exist in many other countries. This stands in stark contrast to the Catholic position that parents are the first educators of their children and should therefore have the full freedom to choose the best form of education for their children, whether such education is state-sponsored or not. We have to recognise that there exists a profound gap between the imposed unitary culture and our Christian tradition.[9] This is a point that will be discussed further when we consider the relationship between Catholic social teaching and public policy. It is worth noting that in many cases Catholic schools themselves—and the Catholic population more widely—have been ill-equipped when it comes to dealing with encroachment by the state on parental autonomy in education. Often the necessary intellectual rigour in political debate, or the inclination to resist that encroachment, is missing.

The above four phenomena are clearly interwoven. In most Western countries, this continues to lead to the state taking over Catholic educational institutions either directly or indirectly by providing state funding with the usual strings attached. The end result is the same, as in both cases the school or university ultimately loses its Catholic identity. What remains of Catholic education can be divided roughly into two groups. On the one hand, there are schools and universities still run by dioceses and religious orders or that have a Catholic character through

---

[9] See Dawson, *Crisis of Western Education*, 112.

some other mechanism approved by a diocese, that can often lack the resources, well-formed personnel and necessary independence from state bureaucracy to retain a strong Catholic identity. On the other hand, there are, increasing in number but still relatively few and generally small, fully independent and privately funded Catholic schools and universities that are thriving because of their clear Catholic identity and curriculum and not despite it.

Whilst not ignoring the many positive results that the development of state-sponsored education accessible for all has brought Western society, we should not remain blind to the serious problems caused by the incessant advance of this system of state-imposed secularism and moral relativism. The state has reached a position where it is not supporting the family and the community in their own initiatives—as would be applauded by Catholic social teaching and many secular groups—but, rather, it is crowding out the initiative of others or directing the educational sector. In his insightful book on Christian education, Douglas Wilson summarises in a nutshell what has gone wrong with education in the Western world in general: It is the enthronement of the misplaced idea that education can or even should take place in a moral vacuum.[10] Education cannot be neutral as to the fundamental principles of human life and the natural order of creation that needs to be understood by the young mind in order to make reasoned decisions in life. Neither can a school be neutral about religion. It either accepts and embraces it, or rejects it.

Catholic education has not been left unaffected by this development, not least because the Catholic Church as such has been deeply affected by the tide of secularism and moral relativism within its own ranks. The decline of Catholic education has in general terms—thankfully there are impressive

---

[10] Wilson, *Recovering the Lost Tools of Learning*, 57–59.

exceptions as well—followed closely on the heels of rising secularism. Over the past decades, established Catholic schools and universities have only in a limited number of cases been able to retain their distinctively Christian character. Very many institutions have, to greater or lesser extent, watered down or thrown overboard altogether their Catholic identity in all but name. As has already been discussed, the secular state has gained ever more influence over the content of Catholic school curricula and school life in exchange for official accreditation and increased funding. At the same time the Catholic Church on the local level has been either unable or unwilling to intervene in order to have schools adhere to the stipulations of *Ex Corde Ecclesiae*, a document promulgated by Blessed John Paul II in an effort to bring formerly Catholic schools and universities back into the fold of the Church. In general, it is relatively newly founded and fully independent Catholic schools and universities that have shown a real commitment to *Ex Corde Ecclesiae*. Most long-established Catholic educational institutions have been unenthusiastic about identifying themselves publicly with Catholic teaching.

Conclusion

It is clear from the above that Western nations currently face a profound crisis in state education as well as in Catholic education, albeit in different forms and with varying intensity. Catholic schools and universities in general seem to have largely lost track of their mission to be places where "we encounter the living God who in Jesus Christ reveals his transforming love and truth."[11] If established schools suffer from low academic standards as well, parents are logically faced with the question

---

[11] Pope Benedict XVI, Address during meeting with Catholic educators, Washington, DC.

of whether sending their children to these schools will be good for them at all. As a consequence, there is an urgent need for new forms of education that are independent of the state and often of the existing institutions of the local Church.

It is sad to say, but in many cases diocesan Church bureaucracy is part of the problem in the decline of Catholic education. This is due to the fact that these structures are often staffed by people who, while well-meaning, are, however, not well-formed in the Catholic faith and tradition and therefore do not possess a sufficiently clear understanding of what Catholic education should entail. Many of them will not be able to tackle the core issues Catholic education is facing today. As we will discuss, the revival in Catholic education is generally not going to come from the local institutional structures within the Catholic Church as such, and even less from the state. As new initiatives throughout Europe and the United States show, Catholic parents who are rooted in the life of the Church will be the driving force behind this renewal. This is a logical development that puts the primary responsibility for education where it belongs. Parental prerogative to educate children is a basic human right enshrined in many international documents (to be discussed in detail below) but all too often forgotten by governments. Schools, whether state or private, are to assist parents, not to take over from them; this is the battle cry of the parent-initiated new school movement. Dioceses will have to take decisions as to whether their education structures need reforming and, if so, how. Meanwhile, as we discuss in chapter 6, dioceses should not place obstacles in the way of new lay (or religious order) initiatives in Catholic education that are rooted in the principles we outline. To do so would be to put the interests of the diocesan bureaucracy ahead of the mission of the Church. The freedom of parents should not be feared as something that will lead to divisions or the rejection of civic responsibility. Indeed, children must be prepared within Catholic schools to go out into the world as Christians because, as Pope Benedict remarked during his 2010 visit to Britain: "The world of reason and the world of faith—the world of secular rationality and the world of religious belief—need one another and should not be afraid to enter into a profound and ongoing dialogue, for the good of our civilization."[12]

---

[12] Pope Benedict XVI, Address at Westminster Hall, London (17 September 2010).

IV Catholic Education and the State: The Foundational Principles of Catholic Social Teaching

The relationship between Catholic education and the state has taken a variety of forms in different countries and at different times in history. However, the "signs of the times" in which we need to think about the application of Catholic social teaching to public policy in education include as perhaps their most prominent feature a major decline in religious practice and a general indifference towards religion, especially in the upper echelons of Western political systems. At the same time, however, there has been a greater recognition in many countries that, for both practical reasons and reasons of principle, parents should have greater autonomy when choosing schools. Expanding opportunities to choose schools, however, has often been accompanied by more extensive regulation of schools.

How should Catholic social teaching approach the question of public policy in education? As in other areas of Catholic teaching on matters to do with political economy, there is no "correct" Catholic answer to the question: "to what extent should the state be involved with education?" However, arguably, more guidance has been given by the Church on this subject than on other controversial political matters. This is largely, of course, because of the relationship among evangelization, education, and the formation of the whole human person and because of the vital role of the family—and especially the parents chosen by God—in both formation and education. Both of these issues have been discussed above. Before considering the Church's statements on education in chapter 6, we will examine the foundations of Catholic social teaching and how they might be relevant to Catholic solutions for education policy; this will be followed by a discussion of practice in some sample countries in chapter 5.

Human Dignity

The Church regards the dignity of the human person as the foundation of all the other principles and content of the Church's social doctrine (*Compendium of the Social Doctrine [CSD]*, no. 160). Man is made in the image and likeness of God and thus receives an inalienable dignity from God Himself (*CSD*, no. 105). Because of the dignity of each human person from the moment of conception "the social order and its development must invariably work to the benefit of the human person, since the order of things is to be subordinate to the order of persons and not the other way round" (*Gaudium et spes*, no. 26). Every political, economic, social, scientific, and cultural programme must be inspired by the awareness of the primacy of each human being over society (*CSD*, no. 132). "In no case, therefore, is the human person to be manipulated for ends foreign to his own development, which can find complete fulfilment only in God and his plan of salvation" (*CSD*, no. 133).

> For this reason neither his life nor the development of his thought, nor his good, nor those who are part of his personal and social activities can be subject to unjust restrictions in the exercise of their rights and freedom. The person cannot be a means for carrying out economic, social or political projects imposed by some authority,

even in the name of an alleged progress of the civil community as a whole. (*CSD*, no. 133)

The human person, the Church argues, is a reasoning, acting being—a responsible subject who forms an integral part of his community. The human person is social by nature and, as we shall see, this has certain implications and imposes certain obligations.

The principle of human dignity also has implications for education. Firstly, because education cannot be separated from the formation of the human person and the development of his vocation—whether secular or religious—restricting basic freedom in education is a restriction on freedom of conscience, the rights of parents, and the freedom of religion more generally. Unduly restricting freedom in education and imposing the state's concept of education on all families would be to subordinate the person to society. In this respect, the right to religious freedom is paramount in the Church's social teaching. People should not be forced to act contrary to their religious convictions (*Dignitatis humanae*, no. 2), and to prevent a family from educating children in the faith would be to do just that.

The Church states that promotion of human dignity does not just require freedom in education; it also implies that all have a right to education. For example, *Gaudium et spes* (no. 26) states:

At the same time, however, there is a growing awareness of the exalted dignity proper to the human person, since he stands above all things, and his rights and duties are universal and inviolable. Therefore, there must be made available to all men everything necessary for leading a life truly human, such as food, clothing, and shelter; the right to choose a state of life freely and to found a family, the right to education, to employment …

This does imply that, if there is insufficient support from a family's own means or from charity or the Church to provide all children with a basic education, then government funds could be used for this purpose. We shall discuss later how this right to education, with finance being provided by the state, can be made compatible with the principle that all must have freedom in education.

These principles have been enunciated also in the Church's specific letters on education. In *Gravissimum educationis* (*GE*, no. 1), for example, it is stated:

> All men of every race, condition and age, since they enjoy the dignity of a human being, have an inalienable right to an education that is in keeping with their ultimate goal, their ability, their sex, and the culture and tradition of their country, and also in harmony with their fraternal association with other peoples in the fostering of true unity and peace on earth.

However, we are warned that this should not be seen merely as a right to a secular education (*GE*, no. 2): "Since all Christians have become by rebirth of water and the Holy Spirit a new creature so that they should be called and should be children of God, they have a right to a Christian education." Clearly, as we shall discuss, such a right would not be fulfilled if a secular education were provided free by the government and the less-well-off lacked the means to obtain a Christian education.

In order to bring these rights to fruition, the Church must have the space to pursue its mission by establishing schools to serve the faithful. As Vatican II puts it:

> Consequently this sacred synod proclaims anew what has already been taught in several documents of the Magisterium, namely: the right of the Church freely to establish and to conduct schools of every type and level. And the council calls to mind that the exercise of a right

of this kind contributes in the highest degree to the protection of freedom of conscience, the rights of parents, as well as to the betterment of culture itself. (*GE*, no. 8)

Whilst the Church institutionally must have the right to establish schools, the freedom to educate children ultimately belongs to parents: "Parents who have the primary and inalienable right and duty to educate their children must enjoy true liberty in their choice of schools" (*GE*, no. 6). This freedom belongs to parents because of our God-given nature and the gift of free will that is given to us:

> The family, since it is a society in its own original right, has the right freely to live its own domestic religious life under the guidance of parents. Parents, moreover, have the right to determine, in accordance with their own religious beliefs, the kind of religious education that their children are to receive. Government, in consequence, must acknowledge the right of parents to make a genuinely free choice of schools and of other means of education, and the use of this freedom of choice is not to be made a reason for imposing unjust burdens on parents, whether directly or indirectly. Besides, the right[s] of parents are violated, if their children are forced to attend lessons or instructions which are not in agreement with their religious beliefs, or if a single system of education, from which all religious formation is excluded, is imposed upon all. (*Dignitatis humanae*, no. 5)

Given that freedom in education is an extension of freedom of conscience and freedom of religion more generally, values that are stated very directly in *Dignitatis humanae*, it is important to note that the Catholic Church is not calling for privileges for Catholic parents and children. In many traditionally Catholic countries (though also in the UK) systems of Catholic education have become intertwined with the provision of free state education more generally. This means that parents can choose a Catholic education that is funded by government on the same basis as secular education. However, this freedom is not necessarily available to all parents. Furthermore, Catholic parents can be limited in their choice of schools to those the state wishes to authorise (with places and the building of new schools often being severely limited). The Catholic Church, in the authentic promotion of its teaching, does not wish to defend such arrangements as privileges. The Church believes that freedom in education should be available to all parents. It is a fundamental human right and should not merely be a special arrangement for Catholics in countries where Catholics are sufficiently numerous.

This point is, perhaps, especially important in the current secular, moral relativist and atheist environment in which we find ourselves in many Western countries. *Dignitatis humanae* boldly proclaims liberty for all and not privileges for the Church. The Church wishes to ensure that all parents can educate their children in accordance with their conscience, as is reflected in article 3, paragraph 26 of the Universal Declaration of Human Rights. The opponents of the Church wish to ensure that all children are educated in the way that those opponents would wish—thus snuffing out freedom for all.[1]

The Common Good

Following on from the promotion of human dignity, Catholic social teaching also demands that public policy promote the

---

[1] For example, the British Humanist Association wishes all taxpayer-funded schools to be secular schools. In effect, therefore, all schools would teach that the only absolute value is that there are no absolute values! Catholics believe in freedom for humanists, but humanists do not believe in freedom for Christians.

"common good." This is often defined as "the sum total of social conditions which allow people, either as groups or as individuals, to reach their fulfilment more fully and more easily."[2] Sometimes the phrase "ensuring human flourishing" is used as a shorthand.

This is not some utilitarian calculus that involves pulling public policy levers to design society to make it a better place in somebody's subjective judgement. In terms of the modern application of the principle to public policy, we should consider the role of the state in the terms indicated by Saint Thomas Aquinas. The individual exists for society *and* the society for the individual. However, every *institution* of society—*and the government is an institution of society and not society itself*—should be oriented towards serving the human person who is subordinate to God. The role of the state must be to serve the family and the community and those associations that develop from the community so that they can flourish. This may involve the government's assisting families in various ways if necessary in financing their education. If other institutions in society provide such financial assistance, the role of government in education may be relatively small. As a minimum, however, laws need to protect property rights and enforce contracts so that it is possible for the Church and other institutions to function effectively and provide education effectively on behalf of families. For example, laws concerning the use of property and land should not inhibit the development of independent educational institutions.[3] Furthermore, laws should never prohibit families from obtaining an education that parents believe is

---

[2] See *Gaudium et spes*, no. 26.

[3] This can be a serious problem in the United Kingdom. An independent educational institution that has not got the approval of the local authority may well find it difficult to obtain permission to use buildings for educational purposes.

appropriate for their children except *in extremis*—that is except where there are well-founded reasons for believing that the education parents are giving to their children will harm the common good.[4] Examples of laws that do prohibit parents' educating their children as they wish include the prohibition on homeschooling in Germany.

The state does not, in general, need to take positive actions in order to promote human flourishing, though there might be some specific situations where it does so. In the field of education, the flourishing of the human person comes ultimately from a Christian education provided by the parents, with responsibility delegated to schools as appropriate. In general, it is for the state to provide the framework whereby this can be brought to fruition.

That it is the family that is the primary vehicle for the promotion of the common good through the education of children has been made clear over and over again by the Church:

> The family is a kind of school of deeper humanity. But if it is to achieve the full flowering of its life and mission, it needs the kindly communion of minds and the joint deliberation of spouses, as well as the painstaking cooperation of parents in the education of their children. The active presence of the father is highly beneficial to their formation. The children, especially the younger among them, need the care of their mother at home. This domestic role of hers must be safely preserved, though the legitimate social progress of women should not be underrated on that account. (*Gaudium et spes*, no. 52)

The role of the state is to provide assistance, where appropriate, to families and the institutions that develop organically

---

4 For example, if it were known that a school were training children for terrorism, the state could—indeed should—take action.

within society. The state should never be allowed to become an obstacle to such family development in freedom.

The notion that families have a primary responsibility for education is not an individualistic philosophy. The role of the family in ensuring the appropriate education of their children, in turn, has social ramifications, as is stated in *Divini illius magistri*: "From this we see the supreme importance of Christian education, not merely for each individual, but for families and for the whole of human society, whose perfection comes from the perfection of the elements that compose it" (no. 8).

Through a proper education, the young can then discern and follow the will of God, contribute to society, follow their vocation and, themselves, ensure that their own children have the same opportunities for human flourishing.

If human flourishing for all is going to be achieved then, as noted, some form of education for all children should be made possible, using government funds if necessary, at least for the less well off. If government funds are to be used to finance education, there may well arise problems of government control of education that are discussed elsewhere in this monograph. If government policy is to be compatible with Catholic social teaching, then it is important that the level of taxes (to finance education and other government objectives) must never prevent the less well off parents from financing an education of their choice for their children; or, alternatively, government funds must be distributed in such a way that parents are able to use such funds to finance an education of their choice for their children. Catholic social teaching has always demanded this explicitly. If education is necessary for human dignity and the common good and the government is to guarantee that education can be obtained, then this education must be such that it conforms to parents' wishes. If that is not the case, government policy would not then be directed towards the needs of the family but government would be imposing its own desires or the agendas of pressure groups on the family and on Christian communities.

Solidarity

We cannot have human flourishing unless there is solidarity—a deep-seated concern for the welfare of others. However, solidarity is not primarily reflected in duties pertaining to the state. Solidarity is not a public policy agenda but an attitude and virtue that is translated into good works. There is a role for the state in the economic sector—including in education as we have indicated—but we should not confuse the duties of the political community with the duty of us all to act freely (individually and collectively) in a spirit of solidarity. As Pope Benedict reiterated in *Caritas in veritate*, quoting from *Sollicitudo rei socialis*: "Solidarity is first and foremost a sense of responsibility on the part of everyone with regard to everyone, and it cannot therefore be merely delegated to the State" (no. 38).

The Church's record in educating the poor and rooting its education within society is indeed exemplary. *The Catholic School on the Threshold of the Third Millennium* summarises the Church's own historical contribution to the promotion of the common good through social action conceived in a way that develops a sense of solidarity within the community. The document then relates this to the challenges of today:

> In the past, the establishment of the majority of Catholic educational institutions has responded to the needs of the socially and economically disadvantaged.... In many parts of the world even today material poverty prevents many youths and children from having access to formal education and adequate human and Christian formation. In other areas new forms of poverty challenge the Catholic school. As in the past, it can come up against situations of incomprehension, mistrust and lack of

material resources. The girls from poor families that were taught by the Ursuline nuns in the 15th Century, the boys that Saint Joseph of Calasanz saw running and shouting through the streets of Rome, those that De la Salle came across in the villages of France, or those that were offered shelter by Don Bosco, can be found again among those who have lost all sense of meaning in life and lack any type of inspiring ideal, those to whom no values are proposed and who do not know the beauty of faith, who come from families which are broken and incapable of love, often living in situations of material and spiritual poverty, slaves to the new idols of a society, which, not infrequently, promises them only a future of unemployment and marginalization. To these new poor the Catholic school turns in a spirit of love. Spurred on by the aim of offering to all, and especially to the poor and marginalized, the opportunity of an education, of training for a job, of human and Christian formation, it can and must find in the context of the old and new forms of poverty that original synthesis of ardour and fervent dedication which is a manifestation of Christ's love for the poor, the humble, the masses seeking for truth. (no. 15)

Out of solidarity, the government may need to respond to sins of omission if they impair human dignity, as has already been indicated. In fact, this is especially neatly put in the English translation of YouCat (the version of the Catechism for young people): "For a person to be able to use his freedom is a fundamental right based on his human dignity. An individual's freedom can be curtailed only if the exercise of his freedom is detrimental to the human dignity and to the freedom of others." It continues in the explanation: "Freedom would be no freedom at all if it were not the freedom to choose what is wrong. It would violate the dignity of a man if we did not re-spect his freedom." Of course, as noted above, this means that parents' freedom with regard to their children's education has to be respected. It means, further, that we should not impose a Catholic education on all children through the actions of government, just as we do not expect a non-Catholic education to be imposed on the children of Catholic parents. Catholics believe in freedom for all and not just privileges for Catholics.

However, the qualifications are important too. If, as a result of a lack of charity or solidarity, some parents cannot afford education then financial provision should be made for them to obtain an education for their children because the Church regards education as necessary for human dignity. This support can be provided in such a way that it is dependent on the means of the parents, and the level of support would, of course, depend on the cost and availability of education in any given country. It is worth noting that, rightly or wrongly, the state provides education in most western countries on a non-means-tested basis.

Subsidiarity

As we have noted, the principle of family and parental autonomy is not an individualistic ethic, though it does point in the direction of the importance of human freedom. The principle of subsidiarity provides guidance as to how the state can fulfil its duties to promote the common good, whilst supporting the individual, the family, and the community in their own endeavours rather than suppressing them. The principle is not just about the promotion of autonomy—and still less about delegation. It demands that, where the government does intervene, it does so in such a way that it *helps* the voluntary community and families achieve *their* legitimate objectives by never supplanting their initiative, only facilitating it. Subsidiarity is not a question of delegation, it is about *facilitating initiative.*

The principle of subsidiarity was not clearly and explicitly articulated until *Quadragesimo anno* (1931)—though the word is not used in that document. For that reason, and perhaps others, it is often downplayed by those who see a substantial role for the state in economic life, including in the provision of education. For example, Longley in Spencer and Chaplin ed. (2009) states:

> There is a simple rule of thumb to test how close such accounts of CST [Catholic Social Teaching] come to being a true version of this teaching—how early, and how often do they mention the common good? If they are mainly concerned to develop and apply the concept, say, of subsidiarity, for instance to justify an argument in favour of small government or against the welfare state, then they are not faithful to the tradition because they do not set the common good as their fundamental governing principle, from first to last.

This view of Longley is common in US academic circles and very common in the United Kingdom as he helped the Bishops of England and Wales draft a widely circulated and high profile document on Catholic social teaching in the mid 1990s. It is, however, a very serious error.

First, the principle of subsidiarity should hardly need stating explicitly because it is implicit in the heart of the teaching of the Catholic Church. It has its roots in the Church's belief in the dignity of the human person and therefore does not need stating as a distinct principle except insofar as it is useful in practical policymaking (see below). Second, Longley is entirely wrong to point to the common good as the "acid test" of whether Catholic social teaching is understood. The Church itself regards the dignity of the human person as the source from which the other principles of Catholic social teaching are derived. If we hold up respect for the dignity of the human person, then the principle of subsidiarity flows naturally.

Indeed, the principle of subsidiarity is woven into the very fabric of *Rerum novarum*. For example it is stated:

> The contention, then, [is] that the civil government should at its option intrude into and exercise intimate control over the family and the household is a great and pernicious error.... In like manner, if within the precincts of the household there occur grave disturbance of mutual rights, public authority should intervene to force each party to yield to the other its proper due; for this is not to deprive citizens of their rights, but justly and properly to safeguard and strengthen them. But the rulers of the commonwealth must go no further; here, nature bids them stop ... If the citizens, if the families on entering into association and fellowship, were to experience hindrance in a commonwealth instead of help, and were to find their rights attacked instead of being upheld, society would rightly be an object of detestation rather than of desire (no. 14).

Thus, the state exists to safeguard all human beings in the exercise of their rights and freedoms and to ensure that they can live in dignity. It does not exist to acquire for itself arbitrary rights over human persons and families. As we have seen, there is a role for the state in education. This role, following on from the principle of subsidiarity facilitates rather than displaces the initiative of the family. This will be developed in more practical terms in chapter 6.

V   Practice in Various Countries

In this section, we examine practice in terms of education policy in various countries. This is not intended to be a compendium of policy as pursued in these countries but, rather, it is an attempt to highlight some of the main aspects of policy as they relate to Catholic social teaching. Two countries that are often regarded as having strong Catholic traditions are included as are two Anglo-Saxon countries (the UK and US) that began with very family centred models of education provision before becoming increasingly centralised. Denmark and Holland also provide interesting examples. The former because it has, at least in theory, allowed significant parental autonomy in a secular environment and the latter because it has a long history of allowing freedom for churches to provide schools financed on the same basis as state schools.

Germany and Austria

Although Germany and Austria have strong cultural, historical, and language links, their systems of education have, in spite of many similarities, a number of important differences. Most important is the legal framework for education. In Germany there is the *Schulpflicht* (the obligation by law for a child aged five through eighteen to attend an accredited school), whereas in Austria there is the more limited *Erziehungspflicht* (the obligation by law for a child aged six through fourteen to receive education within the broad and flexible curricular framework set by the state). In practice this important difference has two main consequences, namely that in Germany homeschooling is strictly forbidden and the founding of private schools is often very complicated, although guaranteed as a constitutional right, whilst in Austria homeschooling is allowed and founding private schools is relatively uncomplicated. Therefore, the Austrian system provides for substantially more freedom in the design of the curriculum. School autonomy is a much-cherished aspect of the Austrian educational system, also with regard to individual state schools.

Both countries have a bilateral treaty with the Holy See that includes the regulation of Catholic educational institutions, their freedoms, state recognition, and funding. The implications of this legal framework are similar in both countries: namely, Catholic parents do have the freedom to send their children to the (Catholic) schools of their choice, whilst having to pay for this from their own pockets. Even though Catholic schools within the state-Church legal framework receive generous government funding for teacher's salaries and some other items, most Catholic schools still need to charge fees for other aspects of the running of schools. Therefore, the freedom of school choice is in practice more limited than it would seem at first observation.

Recently much media attention has been given to the planned founding of a Catholic boys' Gymnasium in Potsdam near Berlin in the state of Brandenburg (formally Eastern Germany). Since 2007, a group of parents close to Opus Dei and organised in an independent educational association have been trying to erect this school but were repeatedly prevented from doing so by the local authorities who argued that such a school would be discriminatory. In reality the politicians and civil servants involved have shown an open hostility to the Catholic Church and especially to Opus Dei. In addition, there is often a fear of competition from the local school authorities that are also responsible for the state schools. After the founding of the school was blocked by three levels of local government, the case finally ended up before Germany's highest administrative court, the *Bundesverwaltungsgericht*. In January 2013, the Court ruled that there existed no legal obstacle preventing the association from going ahead with its plans to start the Catholic boys' school. At the time of this writing, it remains unclear when the school will open its doors due to the fierce resistance that continues from the local authorities.

In Austria, a country with more deeply rooted Church-state cooperation than Germany, Catholic schools have enjoyed good relations with the state and relatively easy access to government funding. Still, the general trend of secularisation and decline of Catholic education as described above has not bypassed Austria. As is the case in most Western countries, few of the schools and universities that have a Catholic name or association have been able to retain a distinctive Catholic identity as proposed by the magisterial tradition. One important reason for this development is state funding.

The 1960 bilateral treaty between Austria and the Holy See provides that teachers' salaries in Catholic schools, including those of religion teachers, are paid for by the Education Ministry. In principle, Catholic schools have the right to turn down teachers proposed by the Ministry that do not share the school's Christian orientation (in Austria, the appointment of school teachers is centralised at the state or federal level). In practice, however, due to the ambiguity of this provision when applied to individual teachers and most Catholic schools' almost complete dependence on state funding, candidates will only be rejected in extreme cases. This has led even to schools with a genuine desire to retain their Catholic identity becoming unable to do so because they have a faculty that consists largely of non-Catholics or of those who no longer practice their faith actively. These developments are exacerbated by the practice of Catholic schools using the state curriculum (which is secular, but not mandatory) and obtaining free textbooks from the state, thus actively introducing the above-described neutral worldview that comes with it. This process has inevitably led to the gradual erosion of the distinctively Catholic character of Catholic schools in Austria. The situation in Germany seems to be similar.

United Kingdom

The United Kingdom has, since 1944, allowed Catholic schools to be state funded. In practice those schools are generally established by the diocese. They also work within a state school system that is heavily based around catchment areas (neighborhoods) and on which there have been strict limits on expansion and the creation of new schools financed by the state. As such, in areas of static or growing population, there has tended to be a "state school monopoly" for non-Catholics and a "Catholic state school monopoly" alongside it for Catholics. There is often intense competition for places at good Catholic schools so that not all Catholics obtain a place at the school of their parents' choice. Within areas of declining population, there tends to be little problem for parents who wish to obtain a Catholic school place but there is still very little choice because new Catholic schools cannot easily be established. There are, more or less, no restrictions on private schools but full fees have to be paid in addition to the taxes used to finance state-funded schools.

On the face of it, therefore, there is freedom for the Church and for parents. However, there is little institutional variety and, until recently, there has been, more or less, no possibility for a new school to be established in response to parental demand (whether Catholic or otherwise). There have also been increasing controls on admissions, examinations, many aspects of the curricula, and sex education.

The position with regard to the provision of schools was liberalised a little under the 1997–2010 Labour government. This liberalisation was extended by the 2010 coalition government and has now been extended with a provision for "free schools" to be established which will receive state funding on a per capita basis. Dioceses could start such free schools (though this is unlikely because of the already existing network of diocesan Catholic schools) and so could groups of parents, foundations, orders, or lay movements.

Indeed, two lay Catholic movements have seriously considered setting up free schools and one of the authors is aware of a group of parents attempting to establish a free school with a Catholic character. Both the lay movements ultimately decided not to establish a free school. One cited various restrictions such as those arising from anti-discrimination legislation not directly related to education that might make it difficult to staff the school with practising Catholics. The other cited limitations on the admissions policies for free schools which prevent a free school from having an intake that is more than 50 percent Catholic. Anecdotal evidence suggests that the parent group is struggling to obtain the support of the diocese and is therefore concerned that a free school it is trying to establish will not be designated "Catholic" by the diocese.

As far as the finance of schooling is concerned, the new arrangement certainly brings the situation one step closer to the requirements of Catholic social teaching. However, as well as the restrictions on admissions policies, free schools must have their curriculum approved by the Secretary of State for Education. Whether Christian approaches to, for example, sex education will be allowed will be determined by the executive power of one individual in the government. The Secretary of State can also bring free schools under central government control if he decides it is appropriate.

On balance, the new policy is probably to be welcomed in that it makes possible initiatives that were previously not permitted without reducing previously permitted opportunities for Catholic education. But there must be concerns, especially if the local ecclesial authorities decide not to support the establishment of schools in areas where there is an existing diocesan school and refuse to designate new schools as Catholic.

The general approach within the Catholic Church in England and Wales (Scotland and Northern Ireland have a separate hierarchy) is not to oppose increasing government interference in education as long as Catholic schools can follow their own approach in areas that are especially sensitive for Catholics (for example, religious education and sex education). However, the problem with this approach is that it puts different subjects in silos and ignores the fact that all education is for the purpose of the formation of the whole human person and should be, as was described in detail above, Christ-centered as a whole. For example, all schools have to follow a nationally mandated curriculum and there are strong governmental controls over qualifications in all state-funded schools.[1]

This certainly leads to problems. For example, all schools have to teach "sex and relationships education,"[2] and this has

---

[1] This is a relatively recent development. Before 1990, the United Kingdom had a strong tradition of excellent independent curricula design and academic and vocational qualifications used by schools that were set by independent institutions such as universities. However, the control by the state on curricula and qualifications is now more or less total.

[2] Despite the alphabetical ordering of those words, it seems that there is a preference to put "sex" before "relationships" in official government documents.

been accepted by the Church as long as Catholic schools can teach what might be termed "Catholic sex education." It was never really questioned by the Catholic education authorities whether Catholic schools should be co-operating with the secularist agenda in teaching this as a distinct subject. Whilst the teaching of the Church (for example, in *Gravissimum Educationis*) is that "a positive and prudent sex education" can and should be offered in Catholic schools, translating a secular curriculum into a curriculum suitable for Catholics is impossible because the former is based on fundamentally different (and erroneous) premises.

Whilst it is possible for Catholic schools to have (more or less) an entirely Catholic intake of students, there is considerable government influence on admissions policies and the way that schools select students. Not only can schools not generally select on the basis of ability, but the ways in which schools can determine who is and who is not a practising Catholic when there is pressure on places is heavily circumscribed. This has led to some serious conflicts in practice (including conflicts between the Church and parents).

The curriculum and qualifications are heavily controlled by government in state-financed schools. There is a "National Curriculum" which is once again being revised, rather than abolished, and a further movement away from independent examining bodies—exacerbating the effect of changes that happened in the early 1990s. There is freedom, however, in subjects such as religious education but not in, for example, history or science.

Denmark

According to a 2008 article in the *Scandinavian Journal of Educational Research*, "The voucher system in Denmark combines unrestricted generous subsidies with substantial autonomy of private schools as to schedule and teaching methods."[3]

Danish vouchers offer up to about 85 percent of the funding typically spent per student at government schools. This model accommodates a wide degree of institutional and educational freedom, allowing schools (including private Catholic ones) to design and shape their curriculum, provided that they offer required minimal instruction in "basic subjects" (Danish, mathematics, and English) at a level comparable with that taught in state schools. Catholic institutions, therefore, are essentially entirely free to set their own curricula (in religious education, for example) and to determine their own admissions policies.

It would appear that this system fulfils the demands of Catholic social teaching with regard to both finance and control. Indeed, it has been commended as a model that could be copied in the United Kingdom by a prominent Catholic involved in the UK's education system. The freedom of institutions is underpinned by a right of families to request that the funds used by local government for their children's education be used as the parents would wish. This circumvents the problem encountered in formal voucher systems where there can be excessive regulation of schools by the secular authorities. Nevertheless, the proportion of children being educated outside state schools in Denmark is small in practice even if appropriate mechanisms exist for parents to exercise choice in theory.

---

[3] Beatrice Schindler Rangvid, "Private School Diversity in Denmark's National Voucher System," *Scandinavian Journal of Educational Research* 52, no. 4 (August 2008), 331–54.

The Netherlands

Dutch schools operate a *de facto* voucher system and have done so since 1917. Indeed, this element of parental choice has its origins in a deliberate desire to accommodate different religious traditions—both Catholics and Protestants—by ensuring that parents were free to have their children attend religious schools.

Although schools in the Netherlands are nominally run independently, the Dutch government has imposed a wide series of controls on these schools: "Today, the Dutch government defines teacher accreditation requirements, fixes salary scales, curtails the firing of teachers, sets the core curriculum, says how much will be spent, makes it illegal to charge tuition over the voucher amount, and prohibits profit-making in voucher schools. In other words, Dutch 'independent' voucher schools have lost their independence."[4] Indeed, Holland appears to impose much greater restrictions upon the freedom of schools than does Denmark.

The creation of new schools is effectively prevented in any area where an existing school serves the relevant religious group. Existing schools can be expanded, but it is very difficult for new schools to be created. As such, autonomy lies not so much at the level of the parent but at the level of the bureaucracy of the churches and ecclesial communities, and the development of schools appropriate for the needs of particular groups of children is not possible.

---

[4] Andrew Coulson: "Why Federal School Vouchers Are a Bad Idea," Cato Institute (April 8, 2006), available at http://www.cato.org/pub_display. php?pub_id=6342.

United States

Education policy in the United States is more complicated compared with most European countries because the US federal system leaves states with wide latitude in deciding most aspects of education policy, such as state school curricula, curriculum standards for private schools, and methods of funding. Certain states and localities have begun experimenting with voucher programmes in an attempt to provide parents with greater choice for the education of their children.

The United States has a long history of legal conflict on issues concerning the separation of church and state. Because voucher programmes often allow parents to finance education for their children at religious schools (including Catholic schools), various secularist organisations have raised legal challenges to these statutes on First Amendment grounds. However, in 2002, the US Supreme Court decided in favour of Ohio's challenged voucher programme, ruling that, since the principal purpose of the vouchers was the provision of education, generally speaking, and did not *force* parents to send their children to Catholic schools, the voucher programme did not constitute a violation of the separation of church and state. Consequently, several jurisdictions have implemented voucher programmes to help fund their students.

The Bush administration's *No Child Left Behind Act*, though it did not create a voucher system, arose in part out of the desire of some federal legislators to create a federal voucher programme. Though the current administration has not further pursued voucher initiatives, there continues to be debate concerning the future of parental school choice at the federal, state, and local levels of government. In general, the lower level of taxes in the US compared with most European countries does provide more opportunity for parents to access private schools at their own cost. However, this is far from ideal.

Summary

Three trends are evident internationally. Systems such as the Dutch system were developed a long time ago and promised much by way of parental autonomy but have seen it eaten away over time. Nevertheless, the basic right to choose a school from a limited range does exist. Parental autonomy is certainly not the key feature of such systems but there is freedom for local Churches and dioceses.

Second, many countries in recent years have developed school choice programmes that give parents considerably greater autonomy. Examples include Chile and Sweden as well as some of the countries discussed above. Within these programmes, there is the possibility of new schools, including religious schools, being created to serve parents and being financed on the same basis as state schools.

At the same time, there has been more regulation of schools, including Catholic schools, across a number of dimensions in many countries. This includes regulation of admissions, employment, sex education, the curriculum, and qualifications. This is problematic. In some respects, this arises from primary legislation that transcends education policy. Given the gradual encroachment by the state, which has undermined the ideals by which some systems were established, when determining the best policy environment for education, it is not just current policy that is important but the ability of schools to be able to resist interference from the state over the long term.

VI The Road Ahead: More Parent, Less State, and a Supporting Church

Returning to the issues of the common good, family autonomy, and human freedom, we can ask "what is the role of the state in education according to Catholic social teaching?" As has been noted, the Church has suggested that there may be a role for government in financing education, especially for the poor because, without a basic level of education, human flourishing is not possible. Essentially, here, the state would be responding to "sins of omission" when individuals and the community do not provide for the poor sufficiently. Beyond this, however, the responsibility for education is firmly placed on parents, the family, the Church, and the community. The important policy issues relate to how the family's responsibility to educate their children is best facilitated.

As we have seen, there are various ways in which Catholic education has come under attack in Western societies. In particular, governments have increasing control of curricula and there is increasing pressure on governments to curtail the independence of Catholic schools and universities. Sometimes this comes under the guise of pressure to remove any state funding for religious schools on the ground that religion should be a private matter and have no connection with state funding (as if religious people are not taxpayers themselves). More directly, it can be an attack on family autonomy arising from the belief that all children in a society should be given the same state-designed curriculum that has no religious grounding and is "worldview neutral." Furthermore, in many countries, there is a state-prescribed national curriculum that may or may not include religious education.

These perspectives are not only attacks on human freedom, but they undermine the Catholic understanding of education as something that involves the whole human person. Education does not consist of a set of facts about science, history, and so on that can be delivered by one set of people in one set of institutions that is then followed by a religious element that is delivered separately. Education is more effective when it involves the education of the whole human person through (most likely) a school-based education[1] that is complementary to family and parish life.

This perspective should not be seen as one that creates divisions within society. It is simply a recognition that the domains of faith, reason, and morality can never be completely separated during the education of children. Indeed, our children must be prepared within our schools to go out into the world. As we have seen, just as there is a danger that Catholic education will be prohibited or restricted there is also a more subtle danger that Catholic schools are expected to take on board an entirely secular agenda, something that is rejected by the Church. As was reiterated in *The Catholic School on the Threshold of the Third Millennium*:

> There is a tendency to forget that education always presupposes and involves a definite concept of man and life. To claim neutrality for schools signifies in practice, more times than not, banning all reference to religion from the cultural and educational field, whereas a correct pedagogical approach ought to be open to the more

---

[1] "School" being broadly defined.

decisive sphere of ultimate objectives, attending not only to "how," but also to "why," overcoming any misunderstanding as regards the claim to neutrality in education, restoring to the educational process the unity which saves it from dispersion amid the meandering of knowledge and acquired facts, and focuses on the human person in his or her integral, transcendent, historical identity. With its educational project inspired by the Gospel, the Catholic school is called to take up this challenge and respond to it in the conviction that "it is only in the mystery of the Word made flesh that the mystery of man truly becomes clear."

Non-Christians of goodwill should not see Catholic schools (or other Christian schools) as a threat or something that separates young Catholics from society as a whole. It is also very clear that the Catholic school must have a great deal of independence from the state—and from other pressures—to pursue a mission that treats the person as a whole and not as separate compartments each of which is educated according to different philosophies.

So, where does this lead us?

Public Policy and Education

As a minimum, but not sufficient, requirement, parents must be allowed at their own expense to educate their children in Christian schools. As has been made clear above, preventing this would be a grave attack on human freedom. In *Divini illius magistri* it is stated:

> [I]n fact, since education consists essentially in preparing man for what he must be and for what he must do here below, in order to attain the sublime end for which he was created, it is clear that there can be no true education which is not wholly directed to man's last end, and that in

> the present order of Providence, since God has revealed Himself to us in the Person of His Only Begotten Son, who alone is "the way, the truth and the life," there can be no ideally perfect education which is not Christian education. (no. 7)

If Christian education is not permitted as a result of children being required to attend secular schools, then children are denied the right to an education in accordance with the freedom of conscience of their parents. Indeed, an attack on Christian education is an attack on the rights of families to provide their children with a Christian upbringing: It is a very serious matter because it is a violation of the fundamental right to religious freedom, enshrined in countless international human rights treaties and national constitutions. Merely permitting Christian education is not ideal but, if there is a reasonably low tax burden on families and imagination and innovation in the provision of education, it can still be possible for most families to educate their children according to their consciences even if they have to finance education themselves. In the United States, for example, Cristo Rey schools provide low cost Catholic education combined with work experience and a large number of Catholic children are educated in Catholic schools with no taxpayer support (though the proportion has declined rapidly in recent decades).[2]

However, Catholic social teaching goes well beyond the suggestion that Christian education should merely be permitted. It strongly and repeatedly emphasizes parental autonomy in terms of school choice. For example, it is said in *The Catholic School on the Threshold of the Third Millennium*:

---

[2] This has happened as the tax burden has increased, though there is no obvious causal link.

A correct relationship between state and school, not only a Catholic school, is based not so much on institutional relations as on the right of each person to receive a suitable education of their free choice. This right is acknowledged according to the principle of subsidiarity. For "The public authority, therefore, whose duty it is to protect and defend the liberty of the citizens, is bound according to the principle of distributive justice to ensure that public subsidies are so allocated that parents are truly free to select schools for their children in accordance with their conscience." In the framework not only of the formal proclamation, but also in the effective exercise of this fundamental human right, in some countries there exists the crucial problem of the juridical and financial recognition of non-state schools. We share John Paul II's earnest hope, expressed yet again recently, that in all democratic countries "concrete steps finally be taken to implement true equality for non-state schools and that it be at the same time respectful of their educational project." (no. 17; internal quotes refer to other Church documents)

We can be more specific about the role of the state, by examining the principle of subsidiairity, which was perhaps most clearly stated in *Quadragesimo anno*:

Just as it is gravely wrong to take from individuals what they can accomplish by their own initiative and industry and give it to the community, so also it is an injustice and at the same time a grave evil and disturbance of right order to assign to a greater and higher association what lesser and subordinate organizations can do. For every social activity ought of its very nature to furnish help to the members of the body social, and never destroy and absorb them. The supreme authority of the State ought, therefore, to let subordinate groups handle matters and concerns of lesser importance, which would otherwise

> dissipate its efforts greatly. Thereby the State will more freely, powerfully, and effectively do all those things that belong to it alone because it alone can do them: directing, watching, urging, restraining, as occasion requires and necessity demands. (nos. 79–80)

Indeed, this statement fits very well with the Church's policy statements in relation to education. Of course, the state alone might be in the best position to help parents, especially less-well-off parents, to purchase an education. The state may also be in the best position to establish a legal framework that imposes certain minimum requirements in state-funded schools—or prohibit certain things such as the teaching of racism or incitement to violence. However, there is no reason for the state to take away from other bodies the actual provision of education. Education can be provided by parents themselves; by mutual and voluntary associations; by charities; by local churches, religious orders, and non-Catholic ecclesial communities; and by commercial organisations. That education can be provided by such organisations is a matter of fact. Therefore, surely, the principle of subisidiarity demands that those organisations should be permitted and assisted if necessary but not displaced.

The message has been put more succinctly in other documents. Catholic social teaching has been explicit over the decades in stating that finance for education should be provided in such a way that parents' wishes are never supplanted and that private, including Church-provided, education is not discriminated against. Such explicit, specific, and consistent treatment of a policy area is, in fact, quite unusual in Catholic social teaching. One example is in the *Catechism of the Catholic Church*. After reiterating that "the right and duty of parents to educate their children are primordial and inalienable" (no. 2221), the *Catechism* continues: "As those responsible for the education of their children, parents have the right *to choose a school for them* which corresponds to their own convictions" (no. 2229). Indeed, the Church goes as far as suggesting that it is an *injustice* for the state not to support attendance at non-state schools to the same extent that it supports attendance at state schools (which, it could be argued, sounds like a call for something like a voucher system as it has become known in the West); that a state monopoly of education offends *justice;* and that the state cannot *merely tolerate* private schools (*CSD*, no. 241, italics added). This is all reinforced by Canon Law which states: "Catholic parents have also the duty and the right to choose those means and institutes which, in their local circumstances, can best promote the Catholic education of their children.... Parents must have a real freedom in their choice of schools."[3]

These statements are, indeed, very bold. But they are also underscored by the United Nations Universal Declaration of Human Rights, paragraph 3, article 26, which states that parents have the prior right to choose the kind of education that is given to their children. The Catholic Church demands this right for all and not just for Catholics. That right cannot be effective unless financial resources are distributed in ways that do not penalise parents financially for their choice of school.

There is suspicion of such freedom in education, even amongst Catholic educationalists—indeed, perhaps especially amongst Catholic educators. The leading UK Catholic education professor of the late twentieth century, Professor Gerald Grace, for example, has stated:

---

[3] Canons 793, 797. The National Catholic Education Association in the United States has supported school choice programmes explicitly. See http://www.ncea.org/data-information/public-policy.

> In 1997 the Catholic Bishops of England and Wales in *The Common Good in Education* gave more reliable guidance: Education is not a commodity to be offered for sale. The distribution of funding solely according to the dictates of market forces is contrary to the Catholic doctrine of the common good.... Against a market imperative of competitive individual survival, they counterpoised the Catholic values of partnership, community networks and professional collegiality.... Professor Stuart Ransom got to the heart of what markets mean in education when he wrote in 1993: "Action in the market is driven by a single common currency—the pursuit of material interests." While market forces have their place in the commercial exchanges of the secular world, their presence in Catholic education has a polluting effect on the spiritual, moral and social purposes of Catholic schools and they should be resisted.[4]

In fact, there are many Catholic education institutions that offer education in return for fees at both the compulsory and higher education level and this has been true throughout the history of the Church. The incorrect conclusion, however, that education should never be offered for sale, arises from the incorrect premise that, when education is exchanged for the payment of fees, action is necessarily driven by the pursuit of material interests. In fact, the development of a materialistic and utilitarian curriculum has been a feature of the socialisation of education in many countries. Giving parents the freedom and the financial resources to choose schools for their children allows them to choose the values that they wish their children's education to reflect.

Whether we describe the process as "The distribution of funding solely according to the dictates of market forces" or

---

[4] Letter to the *Catholic Herald* (June 2009).

not, the distribution of funding by the state to parents who then use that funding to obtain an education for their children is certainly one interpretation of the policy environment that Catholic social teaching demands.

Regulation of Education

Catholic social teaching does propose a role for the state in the regulation of education. For example, *Gravissimum educationis* suggests that it is important that the government ensures that schools prepare children to exercise their civic duties and rights. *Divini illius magistri* talks, quite reasonably, about state involvement where parents refuse to look after their children properly. However, these are roles that require minimal intervention, probably through primary law, rather than detailed regulation and prescription.

In the last two decades, in many countries, there has been increasing state control of the curriculum, admissions policies, the examining system, and sex education without any conspicuous improvements in performance. The Catholic Church believes that all schools should be free to deliver a truly Christian education that puts the development of the human person and his or her intellect and spirituality at its centre. The regulation of education (especially the elements mentioned immediately above) should be just as concerning to Catholic legislators as policy issues concerning the finance of education. Not only should parents be free to choose a school for their children, but also schools should be free to educate children in the way they feel appropriate. Often, there will be appropriate resources provided by the Church and by Catholic associations and schools should be free to use such resources and develop their own curricula.

Church as Supporter—Parent as Prime Educator

The principle of subsidiarity applies, in a sense, to Church authorities too. Recently, in England and Wales, the Catholic Education Service (an agency of the bishops) pointed out that bishops can choose whether to give a school the title "Catholic." However, there is no reason why dioceses should be the sole or even main provider of education that is designated Catholic. Canon Law says: "*If there are no schools* in which an education is provided that is imbued with a Christian spirit, the diocesan bishop has the responsibility of ensuring that such schools are established" (emphasis added). In other words, bishops may establish schools if necessary, but this responsibility is not a reason for putting impediments in the way of parents, lay movements, and other groups who wish to develop a school with a distinctly Catholic character. Bishops have every right to be prudent before allowing new schools to be formally described as "Catholic" but they should not be obstructive.

It is important, therefore, that the parent is at the centre and that Catholic education does not itself become too institutionalised and bureaucratised. It is, in turn, important that Catholic education does not become dominated by schools provided through partnerships between ecclesial authorities and government.[5] At the very least, initiatives by Catholic movements and parents acting freely should not be discouraged. In both Britain and the Netherlands, for example, Catholic schools exist financed by the state but there are strict rules about the

---

[5] Even the US Catholic Bishops' conference has a remarkably "bureaucracy centred" leading page of its website on education. The "key mission relationships" are described as being with: various diocesan offices, national education organisations, governmental bodies, advisory bodies to the education committee, the Vatican and other Bishops' conferences.

establishment of new Catholic schools and, in Britain at least, the vast majority of Catholic schools are run by local dioceses with parents being given negligible choice.

Indeed, in its own statutes, the Church uses language rather similar to that used to define the political concept of subsidiarity: "Among the means of advancing education, Christ's faithful are to consider schools as of great importance, since they are the principal means of *helping* parents to fulfill their role in education" (Code of Canon Law 796 s.1, italics added). This phrasing also makes clear once again that, since formal schooling is about helping parents to educate their children, parents should also have the freedom not to seek such help and home school their children if they feel this is the best for their education.

The Common Good and Competition

One concern among educationalists is the widely held belief that a uniform, state-funded comprehensive system is necessary to prevent social inequality. We should be careful not to trade fundamental parental rights for other values but, in any case, the evidence suggests that education systems with strong state control—for example, those in Britain, and in America at least until recently—produce less equal outcomes and worse outcomes for the poor than systems where more parental autonomy is allowed (for instance, in much of continental Europe). There is a good reason for this. In education systems with strong state control, the better off can improve their children's education by moving house, by paying privately, by using private tutors, or by articulating their needs to the relevant authorities. These options are not generally open for the less-well-off.

Indeed, evidence from educational choice programmes suggests that there should be no concern about the competition that will tend to arise from giving parents freedom. Sahlgren

71

(2011)[6] and Sahlgren (2013)[7] discuss the evidence in great detail. The first of those publications examines the greater educational freedom that has been promoted in Sweden. The second examines the academic studies that have been conducted on education choice programmes around the world. Broadly, the conclusions are as follows:

- In general, greater parental choice in education improves educational quality. The evidence does not suggest that all such programmes have improved quality, but any reduction in quality from greater choice is rare.
- The benefits of parental autonomy are felt dispro-portionately by more disadvantaged groups such as the poor, those from minorities, and those with special educational needs.
- The benefits from greater parental choice accrue just as much to state schools as to the alternative schools to which parents can send their children when they have more choice: the competitive pres-sure improves all schools.

In other words, it is difficult to argue that the common good is not promoted through parental choice or that some groups gain at the expense of others. It would appear that, even con-fining oneself to the narrow metric of academic quality, choice provides better outcomes for all broad social groups.

---

[6] Gabriel H. Sahlgren, "Schooling for Money: Swedish Education Reform and the Role of the Profit Motive," *Economic Affairs* 21, no. 3 (2011): 28–35.

[7] Gabriel H. Sahlgren, *Incentivising Excellence: School Choice and Education Quality* (London, UK: Centre for Market Reform of Education and Institute of Economic Affairs, 2013).

It should be mentioned—though these narrower policy areas are not the main theme of this monograph—that Sahlgren does recommend that the extension of education choice should be combined with other policies. These include the possibility of "differentiated vouchers" whereby the state provides a greater contribution to the cost of education of the less-well-off or of those with certain disadvantages (such as the dominant language being a second language). Also, there might be a role for the government in requiring the publication of information about the performance of schools. These policies would certainly not be in contradiction to Catholic social teaching.

These conclusions with regard to competition were re-affirmed by a landmark article by West and Woessmann (2010) in the *Economic Journal*.[8] Indeed, the results of this study are quite remarkable. They suggest that the competition effect of the existence of Catholic schools—which, until the recent experiments to promote education choice, have tended to provide the main alternative to state schools in many countries—raises standards in both Catholic schools and state schools. Furthermore, the standards are higher despite lower costs and the rise in standards in the state schools occurs despite the fact that the competing Catholic schools tend to attract more intelligent children on average. In addition, because Catholics have tended to value academic education less than Protestants, there is, in fact, some reduction in average educational attainment resulting from a large share of Catholics in a country's population (ignoring all other factors). However, despite this, the competition effect of a large share of Catholics in the population raises standards for all when Catholics are able to

---

[8] Martin R. West and Ludger Wössmann, "'Every Catholic Child in a Catholic School': Historical Resistance to State Schooling, Contemporary Private Competition and Student Achievement Across Countries," *Economic Journal* 120 (August 2010): 229–55.

establish a competing school system. The authors' conclusion is: "Even though Catholics have historically placed less emphasis on education than, for example, Protestants and Jews, ... their opposition to state education in many contexts engendered private school competition that ultimately spurred student achievement."

There should be no fear that Catholic schools—or for that matter any other schools that develop to compete with state schools—should, in general, generate lower standards. Quite the reverse is likely to be the case. Parental autonomy replaces the mantra "equality for all" with that of "flourishing for all," thus recognising the different aptitudes, abilities and characters of different children.

Indeed, the notion of competition is often misunderstood. Competition does not have to be "cutthroat" price competition between profit-making entities that the caricature of some economic models suggests. Although there is no obvious reason why profit-making institutions should be excluded from receiving state funds on the same basis as other institutions, competition is better thought of as a process of discovering the needs of parents and children that institutions of various kinds should be serving.[9] Rather than competition among schools taking place on the basis of price or simplistic metrics, competition is just as likely to be a process that leads to different forms of institutions providing education in a different style and context that is appropriate for different children, whether Catholic or not. Indeed, one of the sad features of education in the United Kingdom is the inability to develop approaches to education that are effective for those with particular educational needs. Frequently such people are simply squeezed into institutions that are designed to suit the "average" child.

---

[9] See, for example, Israel M. Kirzner, *The Meaning of the Market Process* (London, UK: Routledge, 1992).

Of course, if families are allowed to make choices, then they may choose schools in such a way that particular providers become undersubscribed; in turn, this may lead to schools closing. Indeed, there may even be competition between different Catholic schools in a particular locality. Nothing critical is said about this matter in Catholic social teaching. This can be a natural part of the process of ensuring that institutions meet the demands of parents and not the other way round.

Competition, as properly understood, is not a "free for all." It is a process by which those who provide goods and services discover the needs of those who wish to obtain those goods and services and discover new ways of providing for those needs. The normal result of a competitive process is that those institutions that are most successful have their ideas copied by those institutions that are less successful. Only rarely does competition lead to the dramatic exit of an established provider. In our view, competition in education is to be welcomed because, though it may be uncomfortable for institutions at times, it provides an environment that encourages innovation, success, and attentiveness and responsiveness to the needs of parents and their children. Considering the great challenges that face Catholics in the modern world, there is much need for innovative and truly Christ-centred schools and universities that prepare students to face that world with confidence.

With this in mind, although ecclesial authorities might be reluctant to give a school a "Catholic" label because a school already exists in a given area (possibly one under the direction of the diocese), this would impinge on the autonomy of parents. The Church has explicitly stated that there should be no state school monopoly. It is not obvious, given the tenor of Catholic social teaching and Canon Law, why there should be a Catholic school monopoly either. This debate is especially pertinent in the United Kingdom where ecclesial authorities were allowed to start Catholic schools with state support but where further entry is extremely difficult, leading to a situation where in some parts of the country, school places are not well aligned with the demands of parents.

An absence of competition can lead to school systems where bureaucracies simply develop alternative administrative mechanisms to allocate a fixed number of places at better-quality institutions to a selection of winners among a huge number of *competing* parents, leaving the rest disappointed. In other words, an absence of competition between institutions leads instead to intense competition between parents for school places.

VII Conclusion

Considering the arguments discussed above, a number of specific conclusions can be drawn. These principles could be regarded as reasonable policy conclusions, appropriate for most Western countries, given the existing political environment. This is not a blueprint, but a set of ideas to form the basis of reasonable discussion.

- On the whole, money directed through parents via a voucher will be better than direct funding of institutions by the state.

- A legal right for parents to receive funding from the state that would otherwise be spent on their education by the state would be even more robust. Those funds could only be spent on education, which should be defined liberally in primary legislation.

- Tax relief for private schooling will not lead to the full cost of private schooling being met by the state but will at least make it easier for families to be able to afford an education of their choice and is more likely to ensure that the schools parents choose are genuinely independent.

- Catholic dioceses should not regard it as their role to make "compacts" with the state; rather they should defend the autonomy of schools and parents subject to respect for certain general objectives of the state with regard to the education of all citizens. These general objectives should be defined in primary legislation and not be a matter for regulatory discretion and detailed prescription.

- Catholic dioceses should be concerned to ensure freedom when it comes to the qualifications that schools can use as well as in the development of curricula. Catholic dioceses may well play a constructive role—together with universities, professional associations, chambers of commerce, and so on—in developing curricula and qualifications for use in Catholic and other schools.

- Homeschooling should not be discouraged. The role of the government should simply be to ensure that the child is receiving an education. The nature of that education should be loosely defined in primary legislation and not be prescriptively defined in detail.

The minimum requirement of Catholic social teaching is that the state should allow parents to educate their children in the way that they would wish at their own expense. Of course there must be some basic legal restrictions on the form that education takes but such restrictions should be designed to ensure that the child is properly educated to take his place in civil life rather than designed to regulate the content of the education. The legal framework within which education is organised needs to be robust in the face of the potential creeping regulation and arbitrary regulatory preferences of bureaucratic bodies. This is probably best achieved if the rights of parents and a wide definition of education are enforced through primary law, and detailed state regulation only applies to state schools.

However, natural law, the Church and, arguably, the Universal Declaration of Human Rights go further. The state should not discriminate when funding different forms of education. The least-discriminatory approach would be to fund parents directly to obtain an education for their children. It may be appropriate to vary that funding according to the circumstances of the family. This does not guarantee educational freedom for all, but at least it provides a financial framework within which freedom can exist. It should be noted that the Church does not demand special privileges; it demands the same rights for all parents whether Catholic, Protestant, agnostic, or atheist.

To provide freedom to parents via the method through which schools are financed whilst controlling the content of the education which was then provided by nominally independent schools would, of course, not allow the realisation of the parental autonomy that is so important. Regulation of the curriculum, of sex education, and so on can undermine parental freedom just as much as control of financing can. There is growing control of curricula, examination systems, admissions policies, employment policies, and sex education within schools in a number of developed countries. Catholics should be wary of this.

Whilst the Catholic authorities have the power to determine which schools are and are not given the designation "Catholic," this designation should not be unreasonably withheld as long as a school clearly is of a Catholic character. Certainly, that designation should not be withheld in order to protect the position of an existing school when parents are expressing a preference for an alternative. This does not mean that Catholic bishops should be lax about the Catholic ethos of a school when granting and renewing its designation—quite the reverse.

Competition should not be feared by those who have a special concern for the disadvantaged. The evidence suggests that competition raises standards (including in existing institutions), especially amongst the most disadvantaged children. Indeed, competition is best thought of as a process that most effectively discovers the approaches to education that meet the demands of parents and their children whilst providing the best environment for positive innovation and the efficient use of resources. The evidence suggests that competition has the potential to promote the common good, and there is certainly no evidence to the contrary. As such, there are no grounds for objecting to parental freedom based on the principle of solidarity. The policy of parental freedom is, in any case, justified by the prior principles of the protection of the dignity of the human person and freedom of conscience. In the end, Catholic schools and universities have no small task when they truly wish to be places where "we encounter the living God who in Jesus Christ reveals his transforming love and truth."[1] This great task requires great freedom rooted in the inherent dignity of the human person.

---

[1] Pope Benedict XVI, Address during meeting with Catholic educators, Washington, DC (17 April 2008).

References

Church Documents

(All are available at www.vatican.va, unless otherwise noted.)

Benedict XVI. "Blessed Are the Peacemakers." Message of His Holiness Pope Benedict XVI for the Celebration of the World Day of Peace (1 January 2013).

Benedict XVI. Address of His Holiness Benedict XVI, Meeting with the Representatives of British Society, Including the Diplomatic Corps, Politicians, Academics and Business Leaders, Westminster Hall, City of Westminster (17 September 2010).

Benedict XVI. Address of His Holiness Benedict XVI, Meeting with Catholic Educators, Catholic University of America, Washington DC (17 April 2008).

Benedict XVI. Address of His Holiness Benedict XVI to the German Pilgrims Who Had Come to Rome for the Inauguration Ceremony of the Pontificate (25 April 2005).

Paul VI. Apostolic Exhortation *Evangelii Nuntiandi* (1975).

Leo XIII. Encyclical Letter *Rerum Novarum* (1891).

Compendium of the Social Doctrine of the Church (Pontifical Council for Justice and Peace, 2004).

Catechism of the Catholic Church (1993).

Second Vatican Council. *Dignitatis Humanae* (Declaration on Religious Liberty, 1965).

Second Vatican Council. *Gaudium et Spes* (Pastoral Constitution on the Church in the Modern World, 1965).

Second Vatican Council. *Gravissimum Educationis* (Declaration on Christian Education, 1965).

XIII Ordinary General Assembly of the Synod of Bishops (7–28 October 2012), The New Evangelization for the Transmission of the Christian Faith, *Synodus Episcoporum Bulletin* (Holy See Press Office, no. 33: 27 October 2012).

Catholic Bishops' Conference of England and Wales. Pastoral Letter on Catholic Schools (September 2007). Available at http://www.rcsouthwark.co.uk/joint_past_cath_educ_07.htm.

Secondary Literature

Caldecott, Stratford. *Beauty in the Word: Rethinking the Foundations of Education*. Tacoma, WA: Angelico Press, 2012.

Chaput, Charles J. "Catholic Schools and the Christian Mission" (January 30, 2013). Available at http://www.zenit.org.

Coulson, Andrew. "Why Federal School Vouchers Are a Bad Idea." Cato Institute, April 8, 2006. Available at http://www.cato.org/pub_display.php?pub_id=6342.

Dawson, Christopher. *The Crisis of Western Education*. Washington, DC: The Catholic University of America Press, 2010 (1961).

Hancock, Curtis L. *Recovering a Catholic Philosophy of Elementary Education*. Pine Beach, NJ: Newman House Press, 2005.

Kirzner, Israel M. *The Meaning of the Market Process*. London, UK: Routledge, 1992.

O'Brien, Michael D. *A Landscape with Dragons: The Battle for Your Child's Mind*. San Francisco, CA: Ignatius Press, 1998.

O'Brien, Michael D. *Island of the World*. San Francisco, CA: Ignatius Press, 2007.

O'Donoghue, Patrick. *Fit for Mission? Schools: See with His Eyes, Love with His Heart, Share in His Virtues*, expanded ed. London, UK: Catholic Truth Society, 2008.

Pieper, Josef. *The Four Cardinal Virtues*. Notre Dame, IN: University of Notre Dame Press, 1966.

Rangvid, Beatrice Schindler. "Private School Diversity in Denmark's National Voucher System." *Scandinavian Journal of Educational Research* 52, no. 4 (August 2008): 331–54.

Ratzinger, Josef (Pope Benedict XVI). *Jesus of Nazareth: The Infancy Narratives*. New York: Image, 2012.

Rushdoony, R. J. *The Messianic Character of American Education*. Portland, OR: Ross House Books, 1995.

Sahlgren, Gabriel H. *Incentivising Excellence: School Choice and Education Quality*. London, UK: Centre for Market Reform of Education and Institute of Economic Affairs, 2013.

Sahlgren, Gabriel H. "Schooling for Money: Swedish Education Reform and the Role of the Profit Motive." *Economic Affairs* 21, no. 3 (2011): 28–35.

Schall, James V. *Liberal Learning*. Wilmington, DE: ISI Books, 2000.

Stock, Marcus. *Christ at the Centre: Why the Church Provides Catholic Schools*, 2nd ed. London, UK: Catholic Truth Society, 2012.

West, Martin R., and Ludger Wössmann. "'Every Catholic Child in a Catholic School': Historical Resistance to State Schooling, Contemporary Private Competition and Student Achievement Across Countries." *Economic Journal* 120 (August 2010): 229–55.

Wilson, Douglas. Recovering the Lost Tools of Learning: An Approach to Distinctively Christian Education. Wheaton, IL: Crossway Books, 1991.

About the Authors

Christiaan Alting von Geusau grew up in the Netherlands and obtained a degree in Civil Law from the University of Leiden. He also holds a law degree (LL.M.) from the University of Heidelberg in Germany with a specialization in European Law. Alting von Geusau also studied philosophy at Franciscan University of Steubenville in the United States. Having practiced law in Amsterdam and Brussels for seven years until 2004, von Geusau now lives with his family in Austria where he serves as Chief Development Officer at the International Theological Institute, a private Catholic university near Vienna. He was the founding president of the Phoenix Institute Europe Foundation, an educational institution that aims to form young men and women in the classical and Judeo-Christian tradition. In July 2012, he completed "with distinction" his doctoral studies at the University of Vienna, writing on "Human Dignity and the Law in post-War Europe." The work was published in April 2013 by Wolf Publishers in the Netherlands. Alting von Geusau lectures and publishes extensively in the areas of law, philosophy, and education with a special interest in Christian identity and human dignity. He is the founder of the Schola Thomas Morus, a new Catholic Gymnasium near Vienna. He is married with five children and lives in Baden bei Wien.

Philip Booth is Editorial and Programme Director at the Institute of Economic Affairs in London. He also serves as Professor of Insurance and Risk Management at Cass Business School, City University and has been a Fellow of Blackfriars Hall, University of Oxford. He was a Catholic school governor for twenty years. Booth is a Fellow of the Institute of Actuaries and a Fellow of the Royal Statistical Society. He has previously worked in the investment department at insurance company Axa and as a consultant to the Bank of England. He has also worked on a number of projects developing insurance and finance education in Central and Eastern Europe. Edited and coauthored books include *Christian Perspectives on the Financial Crash, Catholic Social Teaching and the Market Economy, The Road to Economic Freedom* (a compilation of the work of a number of Nobel Prize Winners in Economics) and *Investment Mathematics.* Booth is Deputy Editor of *Economic Affairs.*